# *Praise for Visionary Leadership*

"There are myriad books on leadership—but leadership to where? Burt Nanus's *Visionary Leadership* fills an important gap. He teaches and inspires."
— RICHARD LAMM, former governor of Colorado

"At a time when a charged political atmosphere and intense global competition demand vision and strong leadership, this book shows leaders in all sectors how to use a logical process to create and implement a powerful new sense of direction in his or her own organization."
— THE PLANNING FORUM *NETWORK*

"Step by step Nanus shows how to formulate a vision, how to implement it, and how to monitor its progress."
— *ORANGE COUNTY REGISTER*

"Insights as to what leadership must provide if we are to survive the murky, swirling, and threatening currents of change. All leaders, or those wishing to lead, should read *Visionary Leadership*. [Burt Nanus] may teach you how to live your dream."
— *SCHOOL BUSINESS AFFAIRS*

"As the world of business and industry adapts to the many changes and challenges of the '90s, the need for enlightenment and visionary management grows. Burt Nanus, a frequent authority on the art and science of leadership, has put it all together in this how-to guide to "visioning." It is an indispensable roadmap for navigating an achievable vision of purpose, clarity, and success. A necessary addition to every executive's (and bookstore owner's) bookshelf."
— *NAPRA TRADE JOURNAL*

"*Visionary Leadership* is likely to prove the most important management book of the year."
— EDWARD CORNISH, president, World Future Society

"Unlike many of the other leadership books that provide descriptive case examples of leaders with compelling visions and their successful outcomes, Nanus attempts, in *Visionary Leadership*, to outline a process for defining a vision. Most beneficial to leaders who are trying to determine their organizations' direction, as well as organization development practitioners who are providing executive coaching to leaders and working to change an organization's culture."
— *OD Practitioner*

"Good medicine for many of the leaders that are involved in prevention, health promotion, and health reform — whether in work, health care, government, and/or other settings. A great book with tremendous implications, given our era of societal problems and the challenges to develop effective solutions — especially in the broad-scoped arena of health. If you have a vision for a better tomorrow, read this book!"
— *American Journal of Health Promotion*

"If you are a leader or aspiring to be a leader in your organization, this may very well be *the* book for you. For career practitioners, some good ideas here for group and individual career guidance as well as a recommendation to your aspiring business leader clients!"
— *The International Journal of Career Management*

"Nanus, a leader in linking intelligent futures-thinking to effective leadership, speaks with clarity and simplicity."
— *Future Survey*

"Nanus has done the ultimate service for business types: he turns something as slippery as "the vision thing" into something more than a buzzword."
— *USC Business*

# Visionary Leadership

# BURT NANUS

*Foreword by Warren Bennis*

# Visionary Leadership

## Creating a Compelling Sense of Direction for Your Organization

Jossey-Bass Publishers
San Francisco

Substantial discounts on bulk quantities of Jossey-Bass books are
available to corporations, professional associations, and other organizations. For details and discount information, contact the special
sales department at Jossey-Bass Inc., Publishers.
(415) 433–1740; Fax (800) 605–2665.

For sales outside the United States, please contact your local Paramount
Publishing International Office.

Manufactured in the United States of America on Lyons Falls
Pathfinder Tradebook. This paper is acid-free and 100 percent totally
chlorine-free.

**Library of Congress Cataloging-in-Publication Data**
Nanus, Burt.
    Visionary leadership: creating a compelling sense of direction for your
organization/Burt Nanus; foreword by Warren Bennis.
        p.   cm.— (The Jossey-Bass management series)
    Includes bibliographical references and index.
    ISBN 1-55542-460-0
    ISBN 0-7879-0114-8 (paperback)
      1. Leadership.  I. Title.  II. Series.
    HD57.7.N367   1992
    658.4'092—dc20                                          92-18435

Credits are on page 238.

FIRST EDITION
*HB Printing*      10  9  8  7  6  5  4  3
*PB Printing*      10  9  8  7  6  5  4  3  2  1

*The Jossey-Bass*
*Management Series*

Consulting Editors
Organizations and Management

Warren Bennis
*University of Southern California*

Richard O. Mason
*Southern Methodist University*

Ian I. Mitroff
*University of Southern California*

*To Marlene and Leora,*
*and all others who dream*
*of a better world.*

# CONTENTS

# FOREWORD

When I think about the major problems facing our planet today, six issues immediately come to mind:

- The threat of nuclear terrorism
- Worldwide famine and plague
- Global warming and the destruction of the biosphere
- The roiling conflict between nationalism and globalism, as witnessed in the former nations of the Soviet Union and Yugoslavia
- Industrial competitiveness
- The degeneration of U.S. society, as expressed in increasing poverty and violence, declining literacy, and growing racial strife

That's not a surprising list; most of you who are reading this book could probably come up with a similar one. But just below the surface of all these problems—the metaproblem, if you will—is the lack of leadership in our human institutions. That's the rub, dear reader: without strong visionary leadership, the problems mentioned above will fester into a gangrenous deadlock.

A recent article in the *New York Times*, authored by an anonymous bureaucrat, gave an unnerving voice to the leadership crisis in government: "The unequivocal message throughout the federal bureaucracy is that nothing is to be accomplished by this government except the creation of good feelings and the illusion of action. . . . [T]he best and the brightest at my agency and others dutifully exercise caution in substantive matters, avoid action and continually seek another clearance, another authorization, until someone just finally says no. . . . Matters afflicting the current and future well-being of Americans are seen only as nettlesome disruptions that must be calmed, rather than problems that must be solved or responsibilities that must be faced."

If those words only applied to the federal bureaucracy, we could breathe a sigh of relief. But, unfortunately, they also apply to our corporations, our nonprofit agencies, our universities, and our hospitals—in fact, they apply to almost any institution in which human beings get together to work.

At its best, inspired leadership can transform and renew our organizations and can energize and inspire workers and voters who have lost confidence in their ability to face the future. But in a world of increasing complexity and uncertainty, leadership today is more difficult and problematic than ever. In fact, as I write this foreword to Burt Nanus's *Visionary Leadership*, I wonder what's in store for us next. What will be true for us as we career toward the next millennium? A Russian federation? Brussels as the world capital? A European Community of twenty or twenty-five nations, including Croatia? A Yankees' World Series?

Constant change disturbs most leaders and managers. It always has; it always will. Machiavelli's observation that change has no precedent still rings true. But visionary leaders recognize that they—and we—are all children of chaos. Thus they disrupt the status quo, challenge the gospel, and disequilibrate the system in the interest of effecting change that ultimately benefits us all.

Burt Nanus has written a book that fills me with equal amounts of admiration and envy. For the first time ever, Nanus defines for us what "the vision thing" is all about and how it relates to other tasks of leadership. *Visionary Leadership* also provides a step-by-step approach that leaders at any level can use to develop a vision for their organization. Most of all, Nanus describes how to translate vision into action, for action without vision is stumbling in the dark, and vision without action is poverty-stricken poetry. Nanus, in this seminal work, brings it all together.

I wish I had written this book—but I'm forever indebted to Burt Nanus for having the vision to write it.

*July 1992*                                          WARREN BENNIS
*Santa Monica, California*

# INTRODUCTION TO THE PAPERBACK EDITION

In the brief time since the original publication of this book, the importance of visionary leadership has dramatically increased in many fields, from politics and business to non-profits and public agencies. Consider that:

- In the 1992 presidential election, Bill Clinton sold America a "New Democratic" vision and in recent congressional elections, the Republicans, still smarting from the accusation that George Bush lacked a vision, responded with one of their own wrapped up in a new "Contract with America."

- Business leaders are routinely bombarded with questions about their corporate visions at press conferences and stockholder meetings. Read almost any journal article about a business leader these days and you're sure to find some comments on his or her vision.

- Nonprofit organizations desperately seek visionary leaders to redirect their operations in an era of declining government support and burgeoning social needs.

- Every day, thousands of professionals gather at meetings and conferences all over the country to grapple with issues of vision and leadership. A small army of consultants has emerged to facilitate such meetings.

- The search for a compelling vision is not restricted to the United States. For example, this book has already been translated into German, Japanese, Spanish, Greek and Korean editions, and more foreign language editions are in the works.

I've had an opportunity to talk to thousands of leaders about the ideas in this book, either as a speaker at meetings large and small or as a consultant on matters of leadership and vision. In June 1994, I became professor emeritus of management at the University of Southern California to devote even more time to these activities. I've been able to help leaders in all kinds of organizations develop their skills in visionary leadership and have received a wide range of feedback on the ideas in this book.

I've heard nothing in any of these discussions that would lead me to make any changes in the basic concepts presented here. On the contrary, these experiences strongly confirm my original thesis that a shared vision is essential to leadership effectiveness and a powerful force in organizational change. This book explains what vision is and it is indispensable to success in today's world.

The book also provides a practical, step-by-step approach to developing a compelling new sense of direction for your own organization. The approach works. I've used it many times myself, but more important, I've received calls from people in organizations large and small—a giant aerospace corporation, a small midwestern church, a state agency, etc.—

who've adapted these ideas to their own circumstances and found that it works for them as well.

I have been hearing another message as well. It is much better to develop a vision with others than to try to do it all on your own. A group process or "vision retreat" is likely to improve the quality of your vision by bringing a wider range of informed viewpoints and expertise to bear on your search. It will be easier to implement the results when your team has had a hand in the choice of vision and shares responsibility for it. And the search for a shared vision broadens everyone's understanding of the enterprise and strengthens the leadership team, producing long-range benefits for the organization far beyond that of the vision itself.

With this in mind, I've prepared two short companion pieces to this book. The first, called *The Vision Retreat: A Facilitator's Guide*, describes exactly what has to be done to prepare for and conduct a group search for a new vision. Guidance is provided on how to select and invite the participants; what the participants should be asked to do before the meeting; how the meeting should be scheduled; what facilities and arrangements are needed; how to elicit a dialogue on the key issues and move the group toward consensus; and what problems might arise and how to deal with them.

The second publication, called *The Vision Retreat: A Participant's Workbook*, contains all the instructions and materials needed by the people participating in the retreat. Together with this book, these two new publications should greatly simplify the group visioning process for most leaders. Visionary leadership is an idea whose time has certainly come. As you try to apply some of the methods in this book to your own organization, I invite you to share your experiences with me so that together we can learn how to do it better. Just drop me a line at the publisher's address (Dr. Burt Nanus, c/o Management Series Editor, Jossey-Bass Publishers, 350 Sansome Street, San Francisco, California 94104).

May all your visions be grand... and grandly realized.

*Pacific Palisades, California*                                    Burt Nanus
*May 1995*

# PREFACE

Leadership is very much on everyone's mind today. This is not just due to the muddle in Washington — pundits lament the current lack of corporate leadership as foreign competitors move ever more strongly into markets once completely dominated by domestic firms. Cities, churches, schools, courts, hospitals, museums, and other institutions all seem to be sorely in need of the kind of visionary leaders that built them in the first place — leaders who were determined and confident in their sense of direction, unafraid to take risks, bold and courageous, inspiring and uplifting.

Are there people with such leadership skills today? I believe there are many of them. Perhaps you are one. The problem, though, is that leadership is a much more difficult matter these days than it once was. The world is much more complex and confusing, continually reshaping and renewing itself, changing before our very eyes in endless kaleidoscopic variations. But even as it gets tougher to be a leader, it becomes more necessary, for only strong leadership will enable an organization to survive, let alone prosper, in such trying times. Without leadership, an organization is like a lifeboat adrift in turbulent seas with no oars, no compass, no maps — and no hope.

I've been pondering this dilemma — how leadership today is at once more difficult and more necessary — for over a decade. Two of my earlier books explored some ways of dealing with the many issues involved in modern leadership. I also have had many opportunities to talk with leaders in corporations such as Xerox and Motorola, in public agencies such as the U.S. Treasury Department, in hospitals such as Kaiser Permanente, and at important meetings such as those of the National Education Association and the National Governors' Conference.

One question keeps recurring: despite all the tumult and all the problems, are there any practical steps that a leader can take to greatly improve his or her effectiveness? Fortunately, there are. It may not be an easy process, and it is not likely in itself to turn around a hopeless situation, but if there is one thing that can profoundly increase a leader's chance of success, it is developing and sustaining a compelling organizational vision.

How do I know? Successful leaders have told me time and again that vision was the guiding light and driving force for their organizations. Scholars say it was crucial for great political leaders such as Thomas Jefferson and Abraham Lincoln, for great business leaders such as Henry Ford and Alfred P. Sloan, and for a range of other great leaders from Moses to Martin Luther King. In addition, I have personally observed that vision is the primary vehicle by which numerous organizations attempt to renew and redirect themselves.

But that having been said, it is also true that there is no single, infallible path to creating the right vision for your organization. Every leader develops vision in his or her own way, sometimes rationally and objectively, often intuitively and subjectively. Although there have been hundreds of books on leadership and many of them discuss vision as an important ingredient, little guidance for how to develop a vision can be found in that literature or anywhere else. Excellent books on *implementing* vision have been published in the past few years, but these books offer quite limited help in *forming* a vision in the first place.

Why is that? Perhaps it is because many leaders have difficulty explaining how they arrived at their vision. Some even claim to have arrived at their vision mysteriously, in a brilliant flash of insight, almost a revelation. Perhaps so, but it is more likely that such a revelation occurs only to a mind that has already accumulated a great deal of knowledge and understanding about a particular issue or organizational context and that has been ruminating deeply, though perhaps unconsciously, about possible future directions.

I have heard others attribute their vision not to revelation but to serendipity or circumstance. Perhaps a leader was hired by a board of directors that knew exactly what it wanted and hired someone who had done it before, as is often the case in turnaround situations. Or the leader may simply adopt an idea for a vision that is already present and is just waiting for a champion to pick it up and make it happen.

But what about the rest of us, for whom revelation or serendipity is unreliable? Is there anything we can do to design a vision that will serve us and our organizations well? Fortunately, there is, and that is the subject of *Visionary Leadership*.

## BACKGROUND FOR THE BOOK

Certain common elements must not be overlooked when leaders form a vision for an organization. Several years ago, I tried to identify and systematize these elements. I drew on the literature of leadership, strategic management, organizational behavior, and futures research, as well as on my own research and experience as a consultant, to develop a general approach to designing a vision that could be taught in executive-development programs. I also applied these ideas as a consultant to organizations ranging from manufacturing companies and service firms to government agencies, universities, and professional organizations. The result is the approach described in this book, which I now feel confident will work for most leaders. I do not claim that it is the only way, or even the best way, for any particular individual, but it is a practical process that works well in many situations.

## INTENDED AUDIENCE

*Visionary Leadership* starts with the assumption that you already are a leader of an organization or aspire to become one. The organization may be large or small, new or old. It may be in the private sector, the public sector, or the nonprofit sector. You may hold a position at the very top of the organization, or you may head a division or department within a larger organization. Your unit may be the local office of a public agency, a project or program in a research institute, or a department in a hospital. All that matters for the purpose of reading this book is that the organization you lead has some identifiable boundaries within which it is free to operate, some resources at its disposal, and some people in it whose efforts you are expected to lead.

If you have a certain interest or experience in the field of business strategy, the book may provide you, too, with much to ponder, for one of the purposes of vision is to guide and facilitate the strategic-management process. Only after an organization has firmly committed itself to its vision can leaders and managers begin to develop the necessary strategies for turning the vision into reality. Thus, although vision and strategy are not the same, there is no barrier between them. Indeed, readers familiar with the strategy literature will find that some of the very same concerns and even a few of the same methods can be useful in the quest for vision. However, the purpose of vision transcends that of strategy—it goes to the very core of how organizations function and why leadership is so important.

While the book was written specifically for leaders and potential leaders, it will also be of assistance to students of leadership in schools and colleges who need to develop a deeper understanding of the role of vision in leadership and of the many considerations that leaders must weigh when developing realistic and powerful visions. The final chapter, which discusses the role of visionary leadership in twenty-first–century organizations, may be of particular interest to these readers.

## HOW TO READ THIS BOOK

The purpose and challenge of *Visionary Leadership* is to help you develop the right vision for your own organization. The book cannot develop your vision for you, of course, any more than a cookbook can produce a fine roast pheasant, but it can help you understand how to do it and can guide you through the process.

The book presents a step-by-step approach to developing a vision, based on a systematic analysis of the fundamental nature and future prospects of your own organization. This much can be laid out in the straightforward, rational manner of a "how-to" book. But vision also entails looking at your personal values and life purposes. In fact, for many great leaders, personal and organizational visions are one. Such leaders have an innate sense that their life is part of a larger purpose, which is tied to the organization or social movement they lead. To explore this aspect of your personal vision, use every opportunity for critical introspection as you go through this book. Reflect on your own deepest desires, beliefs, and convictions as well as on what you hope to accomplish through your role as leader of an organization.

Consider *Visionary Leadership* as a workbook rather than

a text to be read once and put on a shelf. Perhaps you will benefit most from applying the methods and concepts directly to your own organization as you complete each section. Or you could first read the entire book to get an overview, then try to apply pertinent ideas to your own situation.

The book is designed to be "user friendly" for individual leaders who plan to develop their own vision statements. However, vision development can also be a transactional process: it lends itself well to group participation. I have used parts of this approach many times as a framework for workshops on vision and strategy. The workshops usually last for several days and involve groups ranging in size from twelve to more than twenty participants. The interactions are generally quite spirited and always illuminating and highly valued by the executives who convene the groups. Often the enthusiasm carries over to other activities, broadening the sense of shared vision and facilitating the implementation process. Thus, you will gain much if you can engage others in the vision-forming process.

# OVERVIEW OF THE CONTENTS

The book is divided into three parts. Part One consists of Chapters One and Two, which define vision and explain why it is so important, lay out guidelines for the right vision, and show how such a vision is different from, yet related to, missions, goals, and strategies for your organization.

Part Two describes the mechanics of the vision-forming process itself. It begins by explaining how to assess your current vision, using a sort of vision audit. Chapter Three introduces a case study that will be discussed in the remaining chapters in Part Two. A pet-food manufacturer was chosen as the example because its products are easily understood and its problems are typical of most manufacturing concerns. The concepts of this book, however, apply equally to service companies, nonprofits, and many other types of organizations.

Chapter Four presents guidelines for developing the scope of the vision — that is, making sure the correct questions are being asked. This involves specifying the time frame, the issues, and the stakeholders to which the vision should be addressed and exploring appropriate measures of the vision's success. Chapter Five follows, with a discussion on how to think about the future of your organization in a systematic fashion and how to capture your understanding of the future in a few scenarios that will govern your choice of a vision. Chapter Six shows how to formulate alternative visions and then how to pick the one that is right for you, your organization, and all its constituencies.

Part Three discusses the process of implementing your vision. Chapter Seven focuses on how to translate your vision into reality. Chapters Eight and Nine summarize the lessons of this book, show how to make development of vision a continuing process in your organization, and discuss the evolving role of vision in organizations of the future. Finally, the Appendix at the end of the book illustrates how the process of developing vision can be applied to a typical government agency.

As we set out on this journey, please remember that general principles are just that. Each organization offers unique challenges and opportunities. As the leader of your organization, you understand better than anyone else what the limits are. If something in this book doesn't apply to your situation, don't use it. Experiment. Improvise. In the end, the vision that you support must be totally your own, based on your own best judgment, understanding, and insight. If this book provides some guidance and perhaps a few good ideas, that will be reward enough for the journey.

# ACKNOWLEDGMENTS

Albert Einstein, when asked how he worked, reportedly replied, "I grope." That would be my answer as well, and I'm pleased to be in such exceptional company. But fortunately, I didn't have to grope alone. There are many whose ideas stimulated me, sometimes setting me off in a new direction, occasionally giving me some encouragement that perhaps I had already arrived somewhere important.

Two invaluable guides to my intellectual groping are Warren Bennis and Selwyn Enzer, my colleagues at the University of Southern California. Selwyn Enzer's perceptive ideas on vision and futures studies have shaped my own thinking over the dozen years of our collaboration at the Center for Futures Research, and his thorough review of earlier drafts of this manuscript led to many revisions that helped clarify and sharpen its message. Warren Bennis, by far the most perceptive and prolific scholar of leadership in the world today, taught me and many others much of what we know about leadership and offered great encouragement while this book was being born. I am proud to count both of them as friends and collaborators and hasten to absolve them of any responsibility for the shortcomings of this work.

Many others — far too many to mention — influenced this work through their writings and teachings. To all those individuals, as well as to the leaders of the organizations in which the ideas were tested, and to the many who patiently responded to my queries, I offer the most heartfelt appreciation. Finally, I must thank William Hicks, senior editor of the Jossey-Bass Management Series, whose suggestions on the text were always insightful and useful; and my wife, Marlene, whose patience, support, and love have always been my inspiration.

*Pacific Palisades, California*                                    Burt Nanus
*July 1992*

# THE AUTHOR

BURT NANUS is an independent leadership consultant and professor emeritus of management in the School of Business Administration at the University of Southern California (USC), where he also served for many years as director of research of the USC Leadership Institute. He joined the faculty in 1969 after ten years of business experience as manager of advanced educational techniques in the Univac Division of Sperry Rand Corporation, as senior technical adviser to management at the System Development Corporation, and as president of his own consulting firm, Planning Technology, Inc. Nanus received his undergraduate degree (1957) from the Stevens Institute of Technology in mechanical engineering, his M.S. degree (1959) from the Massachusetts Institute of Technology in industrial management, and his D.B.A. degree (1967) from the University of Southern California.

Nanus has consulted with numerous corporations, universities, and government agencies on the issues of strategy, vision, and leadership. He has also given lectures and short courses on long-range planning and visionary leadership to thousands of executives in the United States, Europe, and Australia. His interest in visionary leadership stems from his years as director of the Center for Futures Research at the University of Southern California, from 1971 to 1987. Many of the programs at the center were supported by major corporations such as AT&T, Atlantic Richfield, Ford, General Electric, Prudential, and Sears Roebuck as part of their efforts to reposition themselves for heavy global competition in the 1990s. In the course of this work, Nanus and his colleagues developed and tested many of the concepts of visionary leadership.

Nanus is author of six books, including the best-selling book *Leaders: The Strategies for Taking Charge* (1985, with Warren Bennis) and *The Leader's Edge: The Seven Keys to Leadership in Turbulent Times* (1989).

# PART ONE

# What Vision Is and Why It Matters

*Part One of Visionary Leadership defines vision, explores its pivotal role in leadership, and suggests a few easy tests to determine whether you need a new vision for your organization. It also discusses how to recognize a good vision when you see one and what to expect on your way to developing one.*

# CHAPTER 1

# Vision:
## The Key to Leadership

Look, look, look to the rainbow.
Follow the fellow who follows the dream.
—**Song sung by Fred Astaire in the film**
***Finian's Rainbow***

*There is no more powerful engine driving an organization toward excellence and long-range success than an attractive, worthwhile, and achievable vision of the future, widely shared.*

That's it! That's the main message of this book; everything else is detail. But the secret of a good soufflé is in the details, and we will have to probe deeply to understand what vision and visionary leadership are, why they are so critical, and precisely how you, as a leader, can develop a compelling vision for the future of your organization.

## VISIONARY LEADERSHIP

There is an old Chinese proverb that says that unless you change direction, you are likely to arrive at where you are headed. In the last two decades, the United States has been headed toward increased dependence on international sources of oil and investment capital, decreased competitiveness in many key industries, and critical weaknesses in such major institutions as education, housing, and health. If the nation's government and corporations continue down this path, the outlook for the next two decades includes lowered standards of living, enormous debt, and great difficulty in defending the American way of life.

If this direction is undesirable, what other directions are possible, and how do we get there? Questions like these have always been the province of great visionary leaders. The visionary leadership of the founding fathers resulted in the Declaration of Independence and the Constitution of the United States. The visionary leadership of Abraham Lincoln eliminated slavery and preserved the Union. The visionary leadership of Andrew Carnegie, J. P. Morgan, John D. Rockefeller, and others built the great industries that enabled this nation to grow and prosper. And thousands of visionary leaders—such as Theodore Roosevelt, Thomas Edison, Susan B. Anthony, Martin Luther King, and many others—provided direction at critical times in U.S. history.

There is no mystery about this. Effective leaders have agendas; they are totally results oriented. They adopt challenging new visions of what is both possible and desirable, communicate their visions, and persuade others to become so committed to these new directions that they are eager to lend their resources and energies to make them happen. In this way, effective leaders build lasting institutions that change the world. As stated in one recent book, "Leaders are pioneers. They are people who venture into unexplored territory. They guide us to new and often unfamiliar destinations. People who take the lead are the foot soldiers in the campaigns for change. . . . The unique reason for having leaders—their differentiating function—is to move us forward. Leaders get us going someplace" (Kouzes and Posner, 1987, p. 32).

This kind of visionary leadership seems to be in short supply today. Consider the following:

■ Due to the large baby boom population, the productive labor force is now large enough to produce all the goods and services needed to support itself, the government, and the "unproductive" population (children, the unemployed, students, and retired people). In the next two to three decades, however, as the baby boomers retire in great numbers, the number of productive workers left in the population will be a smaller fraction of the total. If we had visionary leadership at the national level, we would be investing and saving for that future. Instead, the nation is doing exactly the opposite: consuming beyond its means and accumulating long-term debt at a rapid rate. This means that today's young people face a future in which they will have to support both a larger population of nonproductives *and* the principal and interest on the debt currently being accumulated. In this instance, the lack of visionary leadership hurts an entire generation of Americans and could very well lead to a disastrous decline in the standard of living for everyone.

■ At the same time, the United States is losing competitiveness in industry after industry. With visionary leadership, we might be able to reverse this trend. Many proudly point to our advanced levels of technology and our innovativeness, claiming they are the salvation of the nation's competitive edge. Then why aren't we protecting our position and investing more in high technology? For example, common sense suggests that this is the time to greatly strengthen our educational system in order to produce workers who can innovate and compete in high technology industries. Instead, the inability of politicians to marshal sufficient commitment or resources and a lack of leadership in the educational community itself have led to two decades of steady U.S. educational decline compared to other developed nations.

■ Most major cities already are choking on traffic and air pollution. Still, high rises continue to be built in downtown areas. Where are the visionary leaders who recognize the folly of this and are willing to decentralize the work force, moving it closer to where people live, by taking full advantage of powerful new information technologies?

■ Many businesses are in the hands of managers who do not have a substantial ownership stake in the business. These managers are interested mainly in short-term profit maximization, which increases their bonuses and wins praise on Wall Street. In the absence of visionary leaders dedicated to the future of their companies, strategic planning staffs are cut back, so-called "long-term investments" are deferred or submerged under the banner of cost cutting, and excess funds are used to buy back stock or acquire other companies, adding little to the productive potential of the country.

■ Parents have traditionally served as visionary leaders in the home, but many children today are treated like unwanted nuisances. Even in good homes, children are often unable to get enough attention from either of their hardworking parents, if indeed they are lucky enough to have two. The daily newspapers measure the price of neglected kids in terms of youth gangs, teenage pregnancies, child abuse, adolescent drug and alcohol addiction, and high school dropouts. Yet these very children are the future of the nation, and their decreased ability to function effectively as adults will be sorely felt by companies trying to compete in the twenty-first century.

Many other examples where visionary leadership is missing could be cited. Where are the leaders who could dream great dreams—of national railways to link a nation, of national parks to preserve nature for posterity, of the elimination of poverty and homelessness, of a life of prosperity for all willing to work for it? In the place of visions that inspire hope, there is only the quick fix: a tax cut here, a corporate bailout there, a little "downsizing," and most often nothing but empty words like "kinder, gentler nation" or "new world order" that make a mockery of the very real need for visionary leadership.

It need not be so. Visionary leadership can be developed or at least improved. Indeed, the country's future demands it, our children deserve it, corporations cannot survive without it, and time is running out. There are thousands, perhaps millions, of people already in leadership positions in organizations of all types and sizes—or who aspire to be so shortly. Perhaps you are one of them. If so, the time has come for you to lead the way, to state your vision loud and clear, to put your organization at the leading edge of a renewal that will make the next decade one of optimism and promise for the people who work with you and for the entire country. Vision is your key to leadership, and leadership is the key to organizational success. This book will show you how.

## WHAT IS A VISION?

When you were a kid, did you have a dream of what you wanted to be when you grew up? When you became engaged to be married, did you imagine the life you hoped to build with your intended? If you ever set out to form a new organization, did you have a clear sense of what kind of organization you hoped it would become?

If you answered yes to any of these questions, then you already have a pretty good idea what a vision is and have had some practical experience forming one. You also know how powerful that vision was in motivating your own behavior and shaping your destiny.

These were personal visions, of course. But the same concepts apply—and even more strongly—to your role as a leader of individuals joined together for some common purpose, that is, as the leader of an organization. A leader's vision also inspires action and helps shape the future, but unlike a personal vision, it does so through the powerful effects it has on the people who work for, use, or otherwise have an interest in the leader's organization.

Quite simply, *a vision is a realistic, credible, attractive future for your organization.* It is your articulation of a destination toward which your organization should aim, a future that in important ways is better, more successful, or more desirable for your organization than is the present. The Constitution, for example, is a written description of the founding fathers' vision for the United States, setting a clear direction and defining values but not specifying how to get there.

Vision always deals with the future. Indeed, vision is where tomorrow begins, for it expresses what you and others who share the vision will be working hard to create. Since most people don't take the time to think systematically about the future, those who do—and who base their strategies and actions on their visions—have inordinate power to shape the future. Why else would such great historical figures as Moses, Plato, Jesus, and Karl Marx have had such enormous influence on succeeding generations? As one writer explains: "Themselves under the influence of that which they envisioned, they transformed the nonexistent into the existent, and shattered the reality of their own time with their imaginary images of the future. Thus the open future already operates in the present, shaping itself in advance through these image makers and their images—and they, conversely, focus and enclose the future in advance, for good or for ill" (Polak, 1961, p. 124).

A vision is only an idea or an image of a more desirable future for the organization, but the right vision is an idea so energizing that it in effect jump-starts the future by calling forth the skills, talents, and resources to make it happen. For example, Henry Ford's vision of a widely affordable car and Steve Jobs's vision of a desktop computer for personal use were such powerful ideas that they were instrumental in assembling the investments and creative people necessary to bring them into being. Talented people and investors always want to be where the action is, and the great leaders—the Fords and the Jobses—show them where that is by providing visions of a better tomorrow.

But it is not just the great leaders of vast enterprises who can perform this remarkable feat. Within a few miles of my house are a dozen bookstores, each reflecting the unique vision of its owner. One sells "New Age" books and paraphernalia; a second is a "bookstore coffeehouse" that features thousands of used mystery books, along with assorted pasta and pastries; a third offers fantasy and horror books, as well as T-shirts and movies on the same themes; a fourth specializes in feminist and children's literature and also runs consciousness-raising seminars; a fifth features travel books, maps, globes, and so on. No two are the same. All were at one time no more than a unique vision in the mind of a single individual, who demonstrated the leadership and drive needed to make it happen.

Vision plays an important role not only in the start-up phase of an organization but throughout the organization's entire life cycle. Vision is a signpost pointing the way for all who need to understand what the organization is and where it intends to go. Sooner or later, the time will come when an organization needs redirection or perhaps a complete transformation, and then the first step should always be a new vision, a wake-up call to everyone involved with the organization that fundamental change is needed and is on the way.

Every day, in thousands of organizations, large and small, some leaders at every level can come forward to show the way with compelling new visions. It may be the head of the Atlanta office of a furniture manufacturer who sees a way to increase her market share dramatically by concentrating on large orders from luxury hotels and office buildings. It may be the president of a church who sees how to increase attendance at services by reorienting activities toward single-parent families. It may be the dean of a business school who points the way toward a future graduate program tailored to a large local industry, such as banking or tourism, or to the needs of a particular student group, such as midcareer executives or entrepreneurs. In any corporation, it may be the plant superintendent, the research director, the vice-president for personnel, or any of hundreds of other leaders all over the organization chart who comes up with a new direction to shape the future of his or her unit.

It could not be otherwise, for vision is central to leadership. It is the indispensable tool without which leadership is doomed to failure. To understand why this is so, consider the true nature of leadership in an organization and how vision affects it.

## ROLES OF LEADERSHIP

The nature of leadership was developed at some length in my last book, *The Leader's Edge: The Seven Keys to Leadership in a Turbulent World.* I characterized leadership as follows: "Leaders take charge, make things happen, dream dreams and then translate them into reality. Leaders attract the voluntary commitment of followers, energize them, and transform organizations into new entities with greater potential for survival, growth and excellence. Effective leadership empowers an organization to maximize its contribution to the well-being of its members and the larger society of which it is a part. If managers are known for their skills in solving problems, then leaders are known for being masters in designing and building institutions; they are the architects of the organization's future" (p. 7).

The contours of leadership may stand out in clearest relief when compared to the nature of management. In his brilliant book *On Becoming a Leader,* my colleague Warren Bennis says that leaders "master the context" rather than surrender to it and makes the following distinctions between managers and leaders:

- The manager administers; the leader innovates.
- The manager is a copy; the leader is an original.

- The manager focuses on systems and structure; the leader focuses on people.
- The manager relies on control; the leader inspires trust.
- The manager has a short-range view; the leader has a long-range perspective.
- The manager asks how and when; the leader asks what and why.
- The manager has his eye always on the bottom line; the leader has his eye on the horizon.
- The manager imitates; the leader originates.
- The manager accepts the status quo; the leader challenges it.
- The manager is the classic good soldier; the leader is his own person.
- The manager does things right; the leader does the right thing [Bennis, 1989, p. 45].

This is not to say that one can't be both a good manager and a fine leader. Indeed, many people are elevated to leadership positions only after successful managerial careers, although there are plenty of counterexamples—such as Betty Friedan and H. Ross Perot—to prove that there are other paths to leadership as well. However, the tasks and roles of leaders are different from those of managers, as are their perspectives and skills, their measures of success, and their functions in an organization. In many cases, leadership is a full-time job, and those who try to be both managers and leaders simultaneously often find it quite difficult to do either job very effectively.

To be an effective leader in today's rapidly changing world requires a delicate, fourfold balancing act:

- First, you must be able to relate skillfully to the managers and workers inside your organization who look to you for guidance, encouragement, and motivation.

- Second, you must be able to take full advantage of the external environment and relate skillfully to people outside your organization who are in a position to influence its success (such people may be investors, customers, or members of the board of directors). You must ensure that your organization is well positioned for the market conditions, legal constraints, and other circumstances that affect it.

- Third, you must be able to shape and influence all aspects of the present operations of your organization including the development of products and services, production processes, quality control systems, organizational structures, and information systems.

- Finally, you must be highly skilled in anticipating the future — that is, in assessing and preparing for developments, such as changes in customer tastes, technologies, or the global economy, that are likely to have critical implications for your organization in the coming decade.

If you were to plot these four dimensions — inside and outside environments, present and future domains — you would find yourself, as leader, in the very middle, balancing them all. Figure 1.1 neatly illustrates the four roles critical for effective leadership:

1. *Direction setter.*
"Let's move forward," says the leader. "But which way is that?" ask the people in the organization. The leader selects and articulates the target in the future external environment toward which the organization should direct its energies. This is the meaning of vision. A dramatic recent example is President Gorbachev's attempt to set the Soviet Union on a totally new path after decades of commitment to a failed economic and political system.

To be a good direction setter, you must be able to set a course toward a destination that others will recognize as representing real progress for the organization. Progress may mean a clear step ahead in effectiveness or efficiency. Alternatively,

**Figure 1.1. Leadership Roles.**

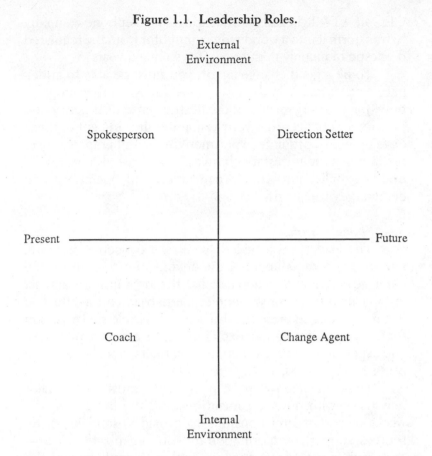

it may mean adding the ability to serve a new set of customers or gaining recognition as the leader in a new technology or product area. If you are successful as a direction setter, you will have established a vision so compelling that everyone in the organization will want to help make it happen.

## 2. *Change agent.*

The leader is responsible for catalyzing changes in the internal environment—for example, in personnel, resources, and facilities—to make the vision achievable in the future. It was in his role as change agent that Charles L. Brown, the

CEO of AT&T, began restructuring the telephone company to transform it into a worldwide competitor from the regulated domestic monopoly it had been for so many years.

To be a good change agent, you must be able to anticipate developments in the outside world, assess their implications for your organization, create the sense of urgency and priority for changes that your vision requires in light of these developments, promote experimentation, and empower people to make the necessary changes. You must also be able to build flexibility into your organization and operations and encourage prudent risk taking.

### 3. Spokesperson.

The leader—as a skilled speaker, a concerned listener, and the very embodiment of the organization's vision—is the chief advocate and negotiator for the organization and its vision with outside constituencies. Perhaps few are as effective in this role as Lee Iacocca, who is a very visible spokesperson for Chrysler Corporation, explaining its intentions, priorities, and expectations to customers and suppliers, stockholders, the press, the Congress, and all the world.

To be an effective spokesperson, you must be the major negotiator with other organizations and the builder of networks of external relationships to provide useful ideas, resources, support, or information for your organization. You—and your vision—must become both the medium and the message that expresses what is worthwhile, attractive, and exciting about the future of your organization.

### 4. Coach.

The leader is a team builder who empowers individuals in the organization and passionately "lives the vision," thereby serving as a mentor and example for those whose efforts are necessary to make the vision become reality. An outstanding example was Martin Luther King, who lived the vision ("I have a dream") and provided a model for everyone in the civil rights movement.

To be an effective coach, you must let people know where you stand, what the vision means to you, and what you will do to make it happen. You must also be committed to the success of everyone in your organization, respecting them, building trust, helping them learn and grow, and teaching them how to constantly improve their ability to achieve the vision.

These four roles—direction setter, change agent, spokesperson, and coach—together define the job of the visionary leader. They are all equally important, and no one can be a successful leader without excelling at all of them. Yet, this is not widely understood. A review of the literature on leadership would show that most of it is devoted to the coaching role. There are endless volumes on the relationship of leaders to followers, on motivation and reward systems, on charisma and the arts of persuasion, on teamwork and trust, on participation and communication and conflict management. These are important, of course, but concentrating on them alone is like an architect caring only about form and forgetting function: the structure might be built and might even be beautiful, but what's it all for?

In short, for leadership to succeed, it needs both form and function, both process and purpose, and that all starts with a clearly articulated vision of the future of the organization. That is what I mean by visionary leadership. But why is vision so powerful a tool for the leader?

## HOW VISION WORKS

A distinguished philosopher once wrote that the greatest force for the advancement of the human species is "a great hope held in common." He went on to say that "everybody knows, without troubling to weigh the reason or importance of a fact seemingly so commonplace, that nothing is more impossible than to inhibit the growth of an idea" (Teilhard de Chardin, [1959] 1964, p. 230).

The right vision for the future of an organization is such an idea. It moves people to action, and because of their action, the organization evolves and makes progress. Since an organization must move forward or, like a bicycle, it will fall over, the role of vision in driving the organization forward is indispensable. The vision's power lies in its ability to grab the attention of those both inside and outside the organization and to focus that attention on a common dream—a sense of direction that both makes sense and provides direction.

Selecting and articulating the right vision, this powerful idea, is the toughest task and the truest test of great leadership. When this is achieved, the organization is already well on its way to the realization of the dream. To understand why, consider the forces that are unleashed:

▪ *The right vision attracts commitment and energizes people.* People seem to need and want something they can commit to, a significant challenge worthy of their best efforts. It is hard to get people to make an emotional investment in the pursuit of another 10¢ a share in quarterly profits. In fact, the only way it can be done is to buy their commitment by pegging their salaries to profits. But that's not what we're talking about here. Vision inspires people by transcending the bottom line. People are willing, even eager, to commit voluntarily and completely to something truly worthwhile, something that will make life better for others, or that represents a significant improvement for their community or country, or that enables their own organization to grow and progress. That's why millions of people volunteer to work for environmental causes, political candidates, and countless charities. But a worthwhile challenge also explains why a firm's scientists and engineers may be willing to work day and night to achieve an important technological breakthrough or why middle managers in some companies are willing to forego their vacations year after year to ensure their firm's success.

■ *The right vision creates meaning in workers' lives.* People need to find meaning in their work, especially in a world where traditional sources of meaning — family, church, community — have been losing their ability to supply a sense of purpose for many people's lives. With a shared vision, individuals can see themselves not just as sales clerks or materials handlers or whatever else their job demands but as part of a first-rate team growing in its ability to provide a valuable human product or service. There is a world of difference in terms of pride, self-image, dedication, and job performance between one worker who, when asked what he does, replies simply "I'm a bricklayer" and another who may have the identical job but answers the same question with "I'm building a home for a family in my community."

■ *The right vision establishes a standard of excellence.* People want to do a good job, to have a feeling that they are effectively advancing the organization's purposes and are being recognized for their contributions. To do so, they have to be clear about what those purposes are and when an action is likely to advance them. The vision calls out to everyone in the organization: "This is what we see as our distinctive competence, this is what we stand for, and there is where we're going." It provides the measure by which workers and managers can evaluate their worth to the organization and by which outsiders can measure the organization's worth to the larger society.

■ *The right vision bridges the present and future.* It is easy to get caught up in the problems and details of everyday work. In a company, the pressures to make a sale or get the product out the door on schedule are often very real and urgent. Competition is keen, crises occur regularly, and investors never seem to tire of demanding increased profits right now — today — or at most, at the end of this quarter. However, the visionary leader knows that the true interests of the investors, as well as those of the firm's managers, workers, customers, and suppliers, are best served by an organization that grows in its ability to serve over time, developing new products and services, improving its quality and operations, and broadening its skills and contributions. The right vision transcends the status quo. It provides the all-important link between what is now taking place and what the organization aspires to build in the future. In doing so, it highlights those present activities that need strengthening if the vision is to be realized. Even in a time of retrenchment, the right long-range vision provides an indispensable guide to what must be preserved and what can be cut back with least risk to future viability.

All of these forces unleashed by the right vision can be summarized in one word that has become the theme for leadership in the 1990s: empowerment. The vision is the beacon, the sense of destination shared by the people who care most about the organization's future. Once people buy into the vision, they possess the authority, that is, they are empowered, to take actions that advance the vision, knowing that such actions will be highly valued and considered legitimate and productive by all those who share the dream.

But suppose there is no vision? Can the organization survive or is it destined to follow the biblical injunction that "where there is no vision, the people perish"? Perhaps there are a few companies in such slowly changing industries that they can go on for years repeating the same tasks and experiences over and over again, caught in a sort of time warp in which habit, ritual, and good management are enough to sustain them for a time, perhaps even a long while. Eventually, however, even the most stable organizations are touched by change, and then a visionary leader must come forward to show the new direction or all is lost.

For most organizations, change and complexity are all too obvious. For these organizations, vision is not a luxury but a necessity; without it, workers drift in confusion or, worse, act at cross-purposes. As the wise old proverb of Italian sailors stated, "Who will not be ruled by the rudder must be ruled by the rock."

In the end, therefore, human behavior in organizations is very much shaped by a shared vision of a better tomorrow. Developing and promulgating such a vision is the highest calling and truest purpose of leadership, for people instinctively "follow the fellow who follows the dream."

# HOW DO YOU KNOW IF YOU NEED A NEW VISION?

At this point, you may be thinking, "Now, wait just a minute. We already have a sense of direction in my organization. We've gotten along fine to this point. What makes you think we need a new vision?" Of course, you may be quite correct, but it might be worth a moment's reflection to see if the time has come to develop a new vision. How would you know? What are the warning signs?

Ask yourself if you are comfortable with the quality of leadership in your organization. There are common warning signs of leadership problems in organizations, and more often than not, such problems can be traced to a lack of direction or uncertainty about the vision. Here are a few warning signs:

1.  Is there evidence of confusion about purpose? For example, are there frequent disagreements among your key people about which customers or clients should have priority, or which services or technologies are the most important to provide, or where the greatest threats and opportunities are likely to be found?

2.  Do your employees complain about insufficient challenge or say they're not having fun anymore? Are they pessimistic about the future or cynical about the present?

**3.** Is the organization losing legitimacy, market position, or its reputation for innovation? Are new competitors emerging who are better serving your customers or constituents?

**4.** Does your organization seem out-of-tune with trends in the environment? Do important outsiders like directors, clients, or investors sometimes suggest that your organization may be slipping or that it's not keeping up with changes in technology or socioeconomic developments?

**5.** Are there signs of a decline in pride within your organization? Are some of your people working only for their paychecks without a real sense of commitment or belonging?

**6.** Is there excessive risk avoidance, with people abiding by their narrow job descriptions, unwilling to accept ownership or responsibility for new projects or resisting change?

**7.** Is there an absence of a shared sense of progress or momentum? Is it difficult for some of your managers to articulate how much things are improving? Do they still feel they have an attractive future with the organization?

**8.** Is there a hyperactive rumor mill, with people constantly trying to find out through the grapevine what is in store for them or the organization? Do people truly trust and respect top management?

If you see one or a few of these warning signs in your organization, then the chances are that the existing sense of direction is either not well communicated or understood or that the vision itself is no longer persuasive or inspiring to people. If so, the time is right to set a new direction for your organization.

# THE CHALLENGE
# OF SETTING A DIRECTION

Developing a compelling sense of direction for your organization isn't necessarily easy, although it sometimes seems so after the fact—especially if the new direction turns out to be so successful that its choice seems obvious in retrospect. But to see how difficult setting a direction is, consider the choices facing leaders of a company encountering stepped-up foreign competition. The leaders may choose to get out of the highly competitive business entirely and invest the firm's resources elsewhere, or they may choose to redouble the firm's efforts in its current businesses, perhaps investing more in marketing, quality, or new product development. Alternatively, they may broaden the product line and diversify. Seeking joint ventures is another possibility, perhaps even with the very firms that are applying the competitive pressures, as General Motors did with Toyota on the Saturn project.

These choices are never clear cut. They are made even more complicated by the cacophony of voices advocating one or another approach, voices that must be heard because they reflect the influential opinions of stockholders, customers, or workers who are needed to help move the company in the chosen direction. Meanwhile, everything in and around the organization is changing: social values, technologies, government regulations, product preferences, tax policies, and all the rest. Rampant complexity, change, and choice conspire to blur images of the future and make the selection of the right vision more complicated, even as it becomes more critical.

So how can a leader know what to do? As this book will demonstrate, it is possible to develop a compelling sense of direction for any organization. The formula for doing so calls for part farsight and part insight, both of which can be enhanced by a systematic and comprehensive study of the organization's present strengths and future prospects.

The process starts with asking the right questions. It then proceeds to develop a deep understanding of all four of the dimensions shown in Figure 1.1: the inside and outside environments and the present and future conditions. It ends not with the selection of the vision itself, as critical as that choice is, but with the acceptance of the vision and the wholehearted commitment to it of everyone involved in shaping the organization's future. Ensuring the vision's acceptance requires all the leader's skills as spokesperson, coach, and change agent.

As Winston Churchill once said, "It is no use saying 'we are doing our best.' You have got to succeed in doing what is necessary." When it comes to leading an organization, there is nothing so necessary as the right vision, widely shared. But how do you know what is the *right* vision, that particular insight that marks where tomorrow begins? Read on.

# CHAPTER 2

# Where Tomorrow Begins:
## Finding the Right Vision

Do not worry about holding high position;
worry rather about playing your proper role.
—CONFUCIUS

Some years ago, when I was serving as director of the University of Southern California's Center for Futures Research, I was visited by a senior executive of a fast-growing food manufacturing company. He said he was concerned about the future of his company. "Are your sales or profits declining?" I asked. "On the contrary," he replied, "they've never been better." "Do you have a problem with marketing or product obsolescence?" I suggested. "No, our product position just seems to be getting stronger each year." "Well, then, are you worried about keeping your technological edge or finding good workers or meeting a challenge from foreign competition?" I wondered. "Not at all," he said, "we're the best in our industry."

"Look here," I finally said with some exasperation, "just what is it that's bothering you?" "Well," he explained, "that's just it. Everything is going so well that I'm getting uneasy. Maybe we've just been lucky until now. Maybe I'm missing something. Or maybe there's something just over the horizon that will clobber us. Besides, when things were tough, I was so busy managing crises that I never had time to think about the future. I used to believe that if everything's going well, leave it alone, or as the old adage says, 'If it ain't broke, don't fix it.' Now I know that's wrong. The best time to try something new, to take risks, to move off in a different direction is in good times, not bad. *Isn't that what leadership is all about—fixing things that aren't broken?*"

Of course, he was right on the mark. The cause of my visitor's concern soon became clear. As a leader, he sensed he might have to provide a new sense of direction for his organization. The old vision, the one originally provided by the founder of the company, had been spectacularly correct and had brought the firm to its current high level of success. But the world was changing, and my visitor wondered whether the original vision would still provide the right direction over the next decade. He was concerned, properly so, with the question "what's next, and why?" He was starting the search for a new vision.

His concern was anything but frivolous. Progress in organizations, like all human progress, is driven by the idealism and optimism captured in a persuasive and appealing vision of the future. In fact, Margaret Mead, the great anthropologist, found this to be a universal human trait, as true for primitive tribes, nomads, and subsistence farmers as for the most industrialized communities in the world. In her own eloquent words: "From comparative materials, it seems quite clear that the utopias men live by are of vital importance in such mundane matters as whether they will struggle to preserve the identity of their society, their class, their religion, or their vocation; whether they will plant trees which take two lifetimes to mature; whether they will take thought to stop the forests from being depleted, the good soil from being washed into the sea, or the gene pool from becoming exposed to too much radiation" (Mead, 1971, p. 44).

But not just any vision will do. Strong leaders want to find that special vision that will shift their organizations into overdrive, that will speed things up in the right direction while conserving energy and power. To be effective, to truly inspire and motivate excellence and achievement in organizations, leaders must find the *right* vision from among the many good and bad possibilities always available. The purpose of this chapter is to provide some guidance in making that choice.

## PROPERTIES OF A GOOD VISION

If your childhood was like mine, you dreaded the inevitable question from well-meaning friends and relatives: "and what do you want to be when you grow up?" How in the world were we supposed to know? When I was small, I didn't even know what the possibilities were. Once I saw a firefighter on a big red truck and immediately that was what I wanted to be. The next week I'd want to be the cowboy I'd seen in a movie or a favorite teacher or a shortstop for the New York Yankees. As I grew older, the images proliferated. I thought about being a lawyer like my Uncle Leon, an astronaut, an architect, the governor of a state, a mathematician, or maybe president of a big company. The trouble was, I hadn't the slightest idea what people really did in those jobs, and I knew there were many other careers I hadn't even heard of.

Images are like that. They explode inside your head and can dazzle and overwhelm you with a collage of apparently limitless possibilities. But of course, most of us never seriously take any steps to become an astronaut or a professional athlete. Most of the images that appear in our brains are recognized as unrealistic, unattainable, uninformed, or undesirable. They soon lose their power to feed our fantasies or motivate our behaviors. They are not the *right* visions, the ones that we expect to make a difference in our lives.

So what are we looking for in a vision? To start with, we need to acknowledge that a vision is a mental model of a future state of a process, a group, or an organization. As such, it deals with a world that exists only in the imagination, a world built upon plausible speculations, fabricated from what we hope are reasonable assumptions about the future, and heavily influenced by our own judgments of what is possible and worthwhile. A vision portrays a fictitious world that cannot be observed or verified in advance and that, in fact, may never become reality. It is a world whose very existence requires an act of faith.

Does this seem too flimsy a fabric upon which to weave our tapestry of intentions? Would you, like many leaders, rather make decisions solely on the basis of history? Consider, then, that history itself is much like a vision—only facing backward. In its own way, history is also a mental model of questionable accuracy and frequent reformulation. After all, the events and people described by the historian no longer exist, and some, like King Arthur and Robin Hood, may never have existed. The mental construct we call history is nearly always based on secondary sources that are woefully fragmented and incomplete. The historian examines a mass of incomplete raw material, selects from among the supposed "facts" those that fit a particular interpretation of events, adds a healthy dose of speculation about all the things that may have happened for which no evidence exists, and tries to weave together a story that purports to tell not just what happened but also why it happened and what resulted.

If you still want to think of history as "reality" you have only to think of any recent public event now fading into history—say, the Kennedy assassination, the Watergate break-in, or the Iran-Contra affair. Despite the minute scrutiny of thousands of distinguished scholars, journalists, and jurists and hundreds of thousands of pages of testimony and interpretation, there are still large domains of uncertainty about exactly what happened in these events, why they occurred, and what their long-range consequences may be. And these were sensational, widely covered, intensely scrutinized events! What about the many developments that are not even noticed today, much less recorded, that will become part of the "factual" record only in retrospect, perhaps a hundred years from now, when historians try to reconstruct what happened in the late twentieth century as we have tried to understand the fall of Rome?

So it is clear that history, like vision, is also a mental model. For all its pretensions to reality, history is heavily conjectural, full of judgments and values, and frequently reflects the historian's desire to influence today's policies. And, as we've just discussed, even our knowledge of the present is necessarily incomplete.

Thus, we may well wonder whether these mental constructs — "history" and "current events" — are really that much more substantial bases on which to act than a plausible vision of the future. From the perspective of leadership, they are not, for compared with history or current events, a vision is a mental construct that we have within our power to transform into reality. In fact, a vision is the only form of mental model that people and organizations can bring into being through their commitment and actions, and therein lies its usefulness and its power.

A second property of all visions is that they are idealistic, what Margaret Mead called utopian. A vision has no power to inspire or energize people and no ability to set a new standard or attract commitment unless it offers a view of the future that is clearly and demonstrably better for the organization, for the people in the organization, and/or for the society within which the organization operates. Often the vision is something entirely new — not a variation on existing activities, not a copy of what some other organization is doing — but something genuinely new, an innovative departure that clearly represents progress and is a step forward. The vision, in short, must be manifestly desirable, a bold and worthy challenge for those who accept it.

So any vision is a mental model of a desirable or idealistic future for the organization. But beyond that, what about the better visions, those that have the ability to renew or transform an organization? Consider Toyota's dream of producing a vehicle — later called the Lexus — engineered to go beyond the existing standards of high-performance luxury automobiles. Or consider Walt Disney's vision, as he described it, for a new kind of amusement park:

> The idea of Disneyland is a simple one. It will be a place for people to find happiness and knowledge. It will be a place for parents and children to spend pleasant times in one another's company: a place for teachers and pupils to discover greater ways of understanding and education. Here the older generation can recapture the nostalgia of days gone by, and the younger generation can savor the challenge of the future. Here will be the wonders of Nature and Man for all to see and understand. Disneyland will be based upon and dedicated to the ideals, the dreams and hard facts that have created America. And it will be uniquely equipped to dramatize these dreams and facts and send them forth as a source of courage and inspiration to all the world.
>
> Disneyland will be something of a fair, an exhibition, a playground, a community center, a museum of living facts, and a showplace of beauty and magic. It will be filled with the accomplishments, the joys and hopes of the world we live in. And it will remind us and show us how to make those wonders part of our own lives [Thomas, 1976, pp. 246–247].

Powerful and transforming visions like these tend to have special properties:

- They are appropriate for the organization and for the times. They fit in terms of the organization's history, culture, and values, are consistent with the organization's present situation, and provide a realistic and informed assessment of what is attainable in the future. This is not to suggest that the organization will not be changed by the vision. It almost certainly will be, perhaps quite radically. But if the vision is not appropriate for the organization, the time, cost, and pain of transformation may be so great as to make implementation of the vision all but impossible. In this case, a totally new organization might be a better choice, as IBM found when it decided to enter the personal computer business.

- They set standards of excellence and reflect high ideals. They depict the organization as a responsible community with a sense of integrity that strengthens and uplifts everyone in it.

- They clarify purpose and direction. They are persuasive and credible in defining what the organization wants to make happen and, therefore, what are legitimate aspirations for people in the organization. They provide agendas that create focus and hold out hope and promise of a better tomorrow.

- They inspire enthusiasm and encourage commitment. They widen the leader's support base by reflecting the needs and aspirations of many stakeholders, transcending differences in race, age, gender, and other demographic characteristics, and drawing stakeholders into a community of concerns about the future of the organization.

- They are well articulated and easily understood. They are unambiguous enough to serve as a guide to strategy and action and to be internalized by those whose efforts are needed to turn the vision into reality.

- They reflect the uniqueness of the organization, its distinctive competence, what it stands for, and what it is able to achieve.

- They are ambitious. They represent undisputed progress and expand the organization's horizons. Often, they call for sacrifice and emotional investment by followers, which are forthcoming because of the inherent attractiveness of the vision.

Visions that have these properties challenge and inspire people in the organization and help align their energies in a common direction. They prevent people being overwhelmed by immediate problems because they help distinguish what is truly important from what is merely interesting. In a sense, these visions program the mind to selectively pay attention to the things that really matter.

Such visions also play a key role in designing the future by serving as the front end of a strategy formulation process. When Toyota articulated its Lexus vision — that is, to produce a new line of cars that exceeded the then-existing standards of high-performance luxury automobiles — it still needed a strategy for attaining the vision. The vision provided the direction, but the strategy provided the framework for getting there. Among other things, the strategy undoubtedly included objectives relating to the intended technical quality and performance of the car, some marketing and production goals, a reformulation of supplier and distribution arrangements, and carefully drawn financial projections.

A good strategy may be indispensable in coordinating management decisions and preparing for contingencies, but a strategy has cohesion and legitimacy only in the context of a clearly articulated and widely shared vision of the future. A strategy is only as good as the vision that guides it, which is why purpose and intentions tend to be more powerful than plans in directing organizational behavior. As Yogi Berra is reported to have said, "If you don't know where you're going, you might end up someplace else."

# WHAT VISION IS NOT

You might conclude from the preceding section that a vision is some sort of magic elixir that cures all organizational ills. This is unfortunately not the case. For every Lexus, there may be a score of Edsels. No matter how well formulated, a vision can fail if it is inappropriate or if it is poorly communicated or implemented. Sometimes visions fail because they were overly ambitious or unrealistic from the start. Sometimes they are overtaken by events and become obsolete before they can be realized.

For a balanced view of what vision can and cannot accomplish, we must be clear on what vision is not:

- While a vision is about the future, it is not a prophecy (although after the fact it may seem so). If I say my vision is to become a great writer, I certainly am not predicting that I will become one, no matter how much my vision may shape my style of writing or my approach to a subject. Although there have been visions so powerful that those who first offered them seem in retrospect to be prophets—for example, Mahatma Gandhi's vision of an independent India or Henry Ford's vision of a car in every garage—these visions had power not because they were prophecies but because of the way they captured the imagination of others, mobilized resources, and reshaped the reality of their times.

- A vision is not a mission. To state that an organization has a mission is to state its purpose, not its direction. For example, the mission of a farmer hasn't changed in thousands of years: it is to grow food and bring it to market at a price that pays for all the costs of production and provides an acceptable standard of living (or profit) for the farmer. However, one particular farmer might have a vision of passing on to his children a farm with twice the acreage he currently has, while another may dream about opening a canning operation on her property, and a third may aim to be a pioneer in growing organic vegetables.

- A vision is not factual. It doesn't exist and may never be realized as originally imagined. It deals not with reality but with possible and desirable futures. It is full of speculation, assumptions, and value judgments. In organizations that depend heavily on the decision-making model of fact gathering, performance measurement, and verification, vision may seem to be an anachronism. But the absence of a factual basis for vision does not necessarily imply a lack of information or substance. As this book will show, visions should be the well-informed results of systematic processes that ensure some degree of comprehensiveness and confidence.

- A vision cannot be true or false. It can be evaluated only relative to other possible directions for the organization. That is, it can be seen as better or worse, more or less rational, safer or riskier, more or less appropriate, or even just good enough.

- A vision is not — or at least should not be — static, enunciated once for all time. The unraveling of the Soviet Union is eloquent testimony to the dangers of staying with a vision — in this case, the Marxist-Leninist ideal — long after it has proven wrong and counterproductive. Rather, vision formulation should be seen as a dynamic process, an integral part of the ongoing task of visionary leadership. Part of the genius of the American system is an electoral process that forces the testing and redevelopment of a vision for the future of the nation every four years.

- A vision is not a constraint on actions, except for those inconsistent with the vision. Instead, it is designed to unleash and then orient the energies of the organization in a common direction, to open up opportunities rather than to restrict them, and to serve as a catalyst for the changes needed to ensure the long-term success of the venture.

Thus far, we have been discussing what vision is, what it is not, and how to tell the difference between good and bad visions. But where does a vision come from? Is it simply a dream born mysteriously in the mind of a leader, a rare stroke of genius, or can it be the result of a considered and systematic process?

# WHERE DOES
# VISION COME FROM?

My wife and I like to travel. Every so often, we'll come to a building or a town square that quite literally stops us in our tracks. It might be a cathedral, an unusual house, or maybe a particularly beautiful park or public monument. As we gaze at the arresting sight, I always wonder, "How in the world did the architect or artist think of that?" After all, where there is now what seems such a perfectly natural and obvious part of the landscape was at one time just an empty lot full of weeds.

Every remarkable artistic achievement starts as nothing more than a dream, usually of one individual, and not infrequently contested and ridiculed by friends and colleagues. Such a dream is a vision not much different from one a leader develops for an organization, for leadership itself is also an art form. Visionary leaders, like artists, are astute and perhaps idiosyncratic observers and interpreters of the real world. Leaders, like artists, try to rearrange the materials at their disposal—that is, the people, processes, and structures of an organization—to create a new and more powerful order that will succeed and endure over time. And the best visionary leaders, like the best artists, are always seeking to communicate directly and viscerally a vision of the world that will resonate with the deepest meanings of people and cause them to embrace it as worthwhile and elevating.

Denise Shekerjian, in an excellent study of forty winners of the Macarthur Award, concluded that the great ideas of these artists, scientists, and social movers and shakers were born of a combination of instinct and judgment. She says: "What intuition provides is an inkling, an itch, a yearning, a mist of possibilities. What judgment provides is structure, assessment, form, purpose. Blend them together—and in the example of Robert Coles [Pulitzer Prize–winning author and child psychiatrist], season this marriage with a strong dose of moral imagination—and you will begin to recognize the tiny, pert buds of opportunity that, if pursued, may well lead to a dramatic flowering of the most creative work of your career" (1990, p. 170).

So where does a leader's vision come from? Vision is composed of one part foresight, one part insight, plenty of imagination and judgment, and often, a healthy dose of chutzpah. It occurs to a well-informed open mind, a mind prepared by a lifetime of learning and experience, one sharply attuned to emerging trends and developments in the world outside of the organization. Creativity certainly plays an important part, but it is a creativity deeply rooted in the reality of the organization and its possibilities.

We mustn't pretend that vision is always the result of an orderly process. It often entails a messy, introspective process difficult to explain even by the person who conceives the vision. Vision formation is not a task for those who shun complexity or who are uncomfortable with ambiguity. Still, there are some basic elements that are part of all attempts to formulate vision, and they are what this book is about. Specifically, they are information, values, frameworks, and insight.

While vision is in a very real sense a dream, it is a special kind of dream built upon information and knowledge. The art of developing an effective vision starts with asking the right questions—and asking lots of them. The next four chapters (in Part Two) identify the questions that need to be asked, what information you need to answer them, and how you can generate that information.

Values are the principles or standards that help people decide what is worthwhile or desirable. They are abstract ideas that embody notions of what truly matters, or should matter, in the performance of an organization and in the ways an organization satisfies its responsibilities to its constituencies—workers, customers, investors, and the rest of society.

Your values as a leader guide your selection of a vision in a variety of ways. Values influence the questions you ask about possible directions. They guide the choice of information you seek to answer the questions and how the information is evaluated. They determine which possible visions you consider, what criteria you use to select among them, and what measures of success you use to judge whether your organization is moving toward its vision. In Chapter Four, you will see how to identify your values and specify your measures of success to help shape a vision for your organization.

Information and values are the raw materials within a structure or framework that allows you to see the big picture. One important part of that framework is your mental model of how your organization and its industry or peer group operates. Another part is a set of scenarios that captures your understanding of how the outside world may change in the future and what implications those changes may have for your organization (discussed in Chapter Five).

It all comes together as a result of synthesis or insight. Sometimes a powerful intuition and drive in the hands of a strong leader are all that is needed. For example, the growth and shape of Southern California is often attributed to Harry Chandler and the Chandler family, who controlled the *Los Angeles Times* and were major landowners in the area. Chandler sensed what would work, decided what would be the best developmental path for Los Angeles and the region, and then simply made it happen. As Halberstam describes it: "They are Chandlers; their bustling prosperous region exists to an uncommon degree because they envisioned it that way. They did not so much foster the growth of Southern California as, more simply, invent it. . . . The city is horizontal instead of vertical because they were rich in land, and horizontal was good for them, good for real estate. There is a port because they dreamed of a port. . . . [Harry Chandler] was a dreamer, and he was always dreaming of the future of Los Angeles, of growth and profit; the commercial future of Los Angeles, tied as it was to the commercial future of Harry Chandler" (1979, p. 136).

Even here, however, one detects a considerable amount of calculation at work, the fruit of analysis and contemplation (if not blatant self-interest) rather than intuition or insight all alone. Intuition is a creative process still somewhat mysterious and poorly understood. However, intuition rarely stands alone and can be assisted by several structured methods, as is shown in Chapter Six.

Finally, the vision must be successfully implemented. As Warren Bennis and I said in an earlier work: "In the end, the leader may be the one who articulates the vision and gives it legitimacy, who expresses the vision in captivating rhetoric that fires the imagination and emotions of followers, who—through the vision—empowers others to make the decisions that get things done. But if the organization is to be successful, the image must grow out of the needs of the entire organization and must be 'claimed' or 'owned' by all the important actors" (1985, p. 109).

There are few things sadder for an organization than an exciting vision that is poorly implemented. Remington Rand, for example, entered the computer business more than forty years ago because it saw the revolutionary potential for such devices. For a short time, it virtually owned the world computer market, but it was a classic case of a great vision poorly implemented. Many years passed before Remington Rand's executives fully accepted the new machine and committed the company to the technical support, marketing, service, and other functions necessary to make computers truly useful for customers. And by the time they did, IBM, which saw the vision much later than Remington Rand but implemented it much better, had obtained an unassailable market advantage. The process of gaining acceptance for a vision and commitment to it is described in Chapter Seven.

To make the discussions in Part Two tangible and easy to follow, I use a particular example throughout Chapters Three through Six. Prime Pet Foods is a division of a large multinational food conglomerate. Its annual sales (largely in North America) of several hundred million dollars represent a small fraction of the parent company's sales. I chose this example for several reasons:

- The product line — dog and cat foods — is simple, prosaic, and typical of many other manufactured products. It would have been easy to choose an example from some "nobler" enterprise — a hospital, perhaps, or a biotechnology company. However, I want to demonstrate that vision is possible even for the most familiar and ordinary of products and organizations.

- The Prime Pet Foods division faces much of the complexity typical for today's firms: intense competition, rapid changes in packaging and product technologies, heavy emphasis on distribution and product positioning, and tight profit margins.

- By searching for the vision of part of a company rather than the entire firm, I hope to demonstrate that vision is both needed and can be developed at many levels.

- Pet food is marketed today like many other products and virtually all services: almost entirely on the basis of intangibles. After all, buyers must choose the product on the basis of claims, promises, and images of blissful dogs and cats without tasting it themselves or getting much feedback from the ultimate four-legged consumer.

The Prime Pet Foods example will allow many business people to follow the discussion more easily. For those in the public sector, the Appendix at the end of the book shows how the same ideas and methods can be applied to a typical public agency, in this case, a State Department of Parks and Recreation. The process would work just as well if the example were another type of organization — a church, perhaps, or a museum, professional association, penitentiary, or any store on Main Street in your town. If the ideas apply across that wide a range of organizations, they probably also apply to yours.

# GETTING STARTED

Let's assume you are setting out to develop a new vision for your organization. Where do you start?

- Learn everything you can about your organization, similar organizations, and your industry. There is no substitute for being well informed on the strengths and vulnerabilities of your own group and on the challenges and opportunities in its environment.

- Bring your major constituencies (for example, customers, investors, the local community, the board of directors, unions, suppliers, and so on) into the visioning process, at first simply through informal conversations and later by soliciting formal suggestions. At a minimum, make sure you completely understand their expectations and needs and the dependence of your organization on their support.

- Keep a playful open mind as you explore the options for a new vision. The correct sense of direction for your organization may be obvious, but don't bet on it! After all, everybody in the industry may be moving in a certain direction, but that doesn't mean it is right for your organization. Indeed, that in itself may be sufficient reason to set off down another path.

- There is no need—and certainly no expectation—that your final choice of vision be your own original idea. Often some of the best ideas for new directions float up from the depths of the organization, but only if they are sought and welcomed when they arrive. Encourage inputs from all your colleagues and subordinates, involve them in the visioning process, and let them know how much you appreciate them all the way through.

- If you are new to the organization, don't disparage the previous leadership or its vision. Everyone knows that you'll be doing some things differently, and they will expect some changes in direction. Instead, show that you understand and appreciate the existing vision, praise your predecessors for bringing the organization to its current stage, and promise to move on, retaining the best of the past but taking full benefit of expected opportunities in the future.

Ultimately, no matter how much help you receive, no matter if the vision was first developed by others and merely adopted and embraced by you, your success as a visionary leader will be measured by the effectiveness of your vision in moving the organization forward. That is what leaders are paid for and, more important, why they are respected and followed.

So now, let's begin. The best place to start is by making sure you have a thorough understanding of the current vision and momentum of your own organization, the subject to which we now turn our attention.

# PART TWO

# Developing the Vision

*The four chapters in Part Two illustrate a systematic approach to developing a new vision for an organization. The process starts with understanding the current status of the organization, then proceeds to drawing the boundaries for the vision, positioning the organization in its future external environment, and finally, to defining and packaging the new vision.*

# CHAPTER 3

# Taking Stock:
## The Vision Audit

I find the great thing in this world is not so
much where we stand, as in what direction
we are moving: To reach the port of heaven,
we must sail sometimes with the wind and
sometimes against it—but we must sail, and
not drift, nor lie at anchor.
—OLIVER WENDELL HOLMES

Wayne Huizenga is a visionary leader who knows how to sail with the wind and how to sail against it. Most important, he knows which way the wind is blowing; you might say he almost smells it. In 1962, at the age of twenty-four, he bought a garbage route in Florida. Six years later, he joined with Dean Buntrock, who had married one of his cousins, to form Waste Management, Inc. To Huizenga, the garbage business was gorgeous, a genuine public necessity being handled by thousands of underappreciated and undercapitalized small firms, each working alone at the local level just when the entire country was becoming environmentally sensitive. He had a vision of a nationwide sanitation company created from many small firms, able to pool their resources, share knowledge, and take advantage of the many new environmental opportunities being created in Washington. Waste Management undertook a blitzkrieg spurt of acquisitions in the early 1970s and is now a $6 billion company, by far the leader in its industry.

Just lucky, you say? Not so, for Huizenga has done it

again and again and again. He built substantial businesses in the bottled water industry, auto parts cleaning, dry cleaning, lawn care, and portable toilet rentals. In each case, he acquired prosaic, undercapitalized local businesses with good cash flows and consolidated them into regional powerhouses. In 1987, sensing a new opportunity in the proliferating ownership of home VCRs, he invested in a small local video rental company called Blockbuster Entertainment and built it into a nation-wide chain of over 1,900 stores, approaching a billion dollars in sales in an unbelievable four years.

Wayne Huizenga is an exceptionally successful leader with an extraordinary sense of vision, but his is a vision always fully grounded in reality. He didn't start Waste Management until he had personally hauled trash from construction sites, run a bulldozer for two years, and managed a small garbage collection firm. He quickly learned a lot about the other businesses, too, so that his vision of what was possible for them was always based on a fundamental understanding of what business scholars call their "core competence." It is no accident that he chose simple businesses, often quite pedestrian, characterized by simple technology, sharp focus, and narrowly defined products and markets. After all, such firms are a lot easier to understand than biotechnology or defense electronics, and Huizenga would be the first to admit that he wouldn't touch a business he doesn't understand.

Since vision starts with understanding the enterprise — or in other words, what you see depends on where you stand — you must be quite clear about the fundamentals of the business you are in. In the following sections, we illustrate this search for the basis of the enterprise with the Prime Pet Foods example, first examining the nature of the business and its mode of operations and ending with a vision audit that identifies where the organization appears to be headed.

# WHAT BUSINESS ARE WE REALLY IN?

An organization is a multidimensional beast. On one level, it can be defined simply by the products or services it provides and the market, customers, or clients who receive them. But there are always other dimensions that sharpen the definition and reveal other facets of an organization's distinctiveness. McDonald's, for example, is so proud of its hamburgers that it calls its training center Hamburger University. Is McDonald's fundamentally just a large chain of hamburger stands? Or is it a giant in the fast-food business or an international franchisor or one of the largest potato and beef processors in the world? It is all of these and more, of course, but the way McDonald's chooses to define its core business influences the directions it will consider possible for its future. For example, if McDonald's defines itself as an international franchisor, then it might make sense for it to open a global chain of pizza outlets—but perhaps less sense for it to buy a soft drink company in Europe or offer frozen Big Macs in supermarkets, both of which would be feasible under another set of definitions.

To define the basic nature of your organization, you need to answer these five questions:

1. What is the current stated mission or purpose of your organization?

2. What value does the organization provide to society?

3. What is the character of the industry or institutional framework within which your organization operates?

4. What is your organization's unique position in that industry or institutional structure?

5. What does it take for your organization to succeed?

These questions may seem obvious or even trivial at first, but it is worth spending the time to ponder them carefully and write down your answers. You should also ask others to do so and check on how much agreement you find. You may be surprised that what seems so obvious to you is seen differently by other people. To illustrate this process, let's go through each question using the Prime Pet Foods example.

### 1.   *What is the current stated mission or purpose of your organization?*

A mission statement defines what the organization has been established to accomplish. For example, in their annual reports, Litton Industries defines itself as "a technology-based company applying advanced electronics products and services to business opportunities in defense, industrial automation, and geophysical markets," and St. Jude Medical is a company that "serves physicians worldwide with high-quality products for cardiovascular and vascular care." Mission statements carefully define products and markets, although some go further to encapsulate management's creed or values, its operating philosophy, or its major goals.

If we look at what the Prime Pet Foods division is doing right now, its implied mission statement would define it as "a company that manufactures a line of dog and cat foods and distributes it to pet owners in North America largely through supermarkets and food chains." Immediately some questions arise that start us thinking about a new vision. Could it produce foods for pets other than dogs and cats? Could it produce more than basic food products for pets, such as vitamins or accessories? Could it distribute through channels other than food chains? Could it market internationally? For now, we simply note these questions and move on.

### 2.   *What value does the organization provide to society?*

Every organization exists within an institutional fabric, deriving its legitimacy from the services it provides to other institutions and to society in general. For example, a church ministers to the spiritual needs of the community, in exchange for which it receives financial and service contributions from its members and certain privileges from society, such as tax benefits and the freedom to espouse or practice doctrines that may be at odds with those of other faiths. Blockbuster Entertainment provides low-cost home entertainment to millions of people who rent their videotapes. It also supports the film industry by providing secondary distribution of films no longer profitable to distribute through movie theaters.

In the case of Prime Pet Foods, the company's service to society is a little less direct. People own pets for a variety of reasons: for companionship, comfort, and security; as a source of diversion or exercise; to give their children a sense of responsibility; or to perform useful tasks (for example, Seeing Eye dogs and cats that catch mice). Pet owners often have an emotional investment in their pets and are concerned about their pet's health and vitality, one aspect of which is a proper diet.

Thus, the value that the company provides to society is the provision of safe, nutritious, reasonably priced pet foods. From the perspective of vision, the obvious question is whether the company should consider broadening its product line to include other products and services that contribute to pet health and vitality, such as medicines or food supplements.

### 3. *What is the character of the industry or institutional framework within which your organization operates?*

Each organization operates in a particular organizational setting. A hospital in a large city, for example, is part of the city's health care delivery system that includes other hospitals, physicians, patients, health insurance companies, the pharmaceutical and medical equipment industries, ambulance services, and so forth. When you start to examine the institutional context of your organization, you may be amazed to discover how complex it is.

Prime Pet Foods is part of a large industry. Pet foods are a big business in North America, ranking right up there with the best-selling items in supermarkets. Approximately 37 percent of all U.S. households owned dogs in 1990. This figure is down slightly from 40.5 percent in 1982, even though the number of dogs owned increased from forty-eight to fifty-four million in that period. About 31 percent of households owned some sixty-three million cats in 1990, up from forty-four million in 1982. Sales of dog food totaled $3.4 billion in 1989, while cat food sales were $2.3 billion. But the dollar sales of cat foods over the preceding eight years increased about 6 percent per year, more than twice the rate of increase in dog food sales. Overall the pet food market has been increasing about 4 percent per year (*Pet Food Institute Fact Sheet*, 1990, 1991). The industry employs some sixteen thousand people. Most of the approximately 250 businesses in the industry are local and quite small, but the industry is dominated by two giants — Ralston Purina and Hartz Mountain, with each shipping over a billion dollars a year in pet foods — and a few others whose sales are in the 300–600 million dollars a year range (*Manufacturing U.S.A.*, 1989, p. 74).

In general, pet food products are sold in four categories: dry, canned, semimoist, and treats. All are some mix of grains, vegetable, meat by-products, and a variety of chemical additives to improve palatability, attractiveness, shelf life, or nutrition. A great variety of products is offered, differing on the formula used, special flavors offered (for example, liver, stew, or tuna), and targeted market segments (for example, gourmet or puppy foods). The largest sales categories are dry dog foods and canned cat foods, which together represent more than half of total pet food sales. Prime Pet Foods competes in all categories with several highly advertised brands.

Despite its substantial sales volume, Prime Pet Foods is a small division of a much larger food company. Its parent company produces and markets a wide variety of food products all around the globe, under hundreds of brand names. About 4 percent of the parent company's total sales is in pet foods, and Prime, which markets only in the United States and Canada, represents less than a quarter of that (though it represents somewhat more in profit contribution). Because Prime Pet Foods is relatively small, it has considerable operating autonomy.

### 4. What is your organization's unique position in that industry or institutional structure?

Each organization needs at least one unique characteristic that defines it, sets it apart from its peer group, and gives it a competitive edge. The organization may have a distinctive competence — that is, something it does better than anyone else — like the operator service provided by AT&T. It may have unique assets, like the great paintings in the Metropolitan Museum of Art, a strong patent position such as Polaroid had with the quick-developing camera, a well-established brand name like Coca-Cola, a fine distribution network like Turner Broadcasting, or perhaps exceptional supplier or customer relations. Whatever it is, a unique characteristic helps define the organization and guides its destiny.

Prime Pet Foods has several unique strengths. It has strong, heavily advertised brand names for its products. Its parent company can provide it with high-quality research and financial resources necessary for expansion and growth, as well as a global presence that makes international marketing of its product line a distinct possibility for the future. Finally, it has a long history of excellent supplier relations.

### 5. What does it take for your organization to succeed?

Every organization has several critical success factors, those factors where excellence is required if the organization is to succeed. For the American National Red Cross, the number of blood donors the organization attracts each year is a critical success factor. For Apple Computer, Inc., superiority in hardware and software design for personal computers is a critical factor.

In the case of Prime Pet Foods, the critical success factors are brand name recognition, supermarket shelf space, product value (that is, low-cost and high-quality), and marketing research.

Thus far, we have been trying to understand the nature of the organization's enterprise. Some clues to possible new directions for a vision have already surfaced in this process. The next step is to look at how the organization functions.

# HOW DO WE OPERATE?

Organizations are all unique in some sense. They tend to feel and act differently even if they're in the same industry or right next door to each other. A new vision may not be acceptable — or may not have the power to inspire action — if it doesn't seem to fit in with the organization's basic assumptions, paradigms, and values. Indeed, such a mismatch is one of the most frequent causes of resistance to change.

Furthermore, the way an organization operates casts a long shadow over both present and future possibilities. Legends, traditions, and habits tend to persist for a long time and determine the organizational culture—that is, "how we do things around here." Past visions often continue to influence present behaviors and may have a certain nostalgic attraction that makes them difficult to dislodge. For example, Polaroid, Disney, and McDonald's are still heavily influenced by the visions of their founders (Edwin Land, Walt Disney, and Ray Kroc) long after these men passed their leadership mantles on to their successors.

To understand how your organization operates, you need to ask these three questions:

1. What are the values and the organizational culture that govern behavior and decision making?

2. What are the operating strengths and weaknesses of the organization?

**3.** What is the current strategy, and can it be defended?

Again, you should write down the answers to these questions after consulting with your colleagues. The following discussion illustrates this process using the Prime Pet Foods example.

### 1. *What are the values and the organizational culture that govern behavior and decision making?*

Values are abstract ideas that influence thinking and action in the organization and, ultimately, the choice of vision. Here are a few examples of values:

- Competition is good; winning is better.

- Seniority should count in who gets promoted.

- Each worker owes a full day's work for a full day's pay.

- People should participate in decisions that affect them.

- The customer is always right.

Values affect vision in several ways. First, values provide the context within which issues are identified and alternative goals evaluated. For example, Jaguar, Volvo, and Maserati are all in the same industry, but their values are so different that it is not surprising that they have different goals for their cars and emphasize different qualities, like design, safety, and speed. Values also shape assumptions about the future and limit the range of choices considered for a new vision. For example, a company may choose to operate in an environmentally responsible manner, thereby eliminating certain product or market possibilities.

Organizational culture includes values but goes further to encompass other dimensions that determine how people act in the organization, for example, beliefs, expectations, norms, rituals, communication patterns, symbols, heroes, and reward structures. In essence, the culture is the present incarnation of all that has gone before: the successes, failures, habits, and lessons learned. In this sense, culture constitutes an organizational memory, which not only guides behavior but provides a sense of identity, stability, and organizational boundaries. Consider how the radically different cultures of the Mafia, a police department, and the Salvation Army determine how people in each organization will act toward each other and the outside world.

Leaders must always understand their own values, as well as the values and culture prevailing in their organizations, because these values determine whether a new sense of direction will be enthusiastically embraced, reluctantly accepted, or rejected as inappropriate. Values and cultures are deeply rooted, persistent, and often constrain possible new directions.

Some of the values in the Prime Pet Foods division include the following:

- Customer satisfaction is the key to everything else. Satisfying the needs and wants of pet owners is the division's first responsibility, and this value drives all other decisions.

- The division must provide adequate returns on investment to the parent company and should continually plan to improve its ability to do so in the future.

- The division should be aggressively competitive. Because competition is so intense, Prime Pet Foods must continually strive to reduce costs.

- Supermarkets must be treated well (for example, they should be ensured of satisfactory profit margins and promotion) since they determine the shelf space granted to Prime's products.

- The division should respect its employees, pay them a competitive wage, encourage their suggestions, and maintain safe working conditions. Employees should be rewarded for good performance and for exceptional contributions to the company's competitive edge.

- Loyalty is highly valued, and promotion should be largely from within. Those who aspire to higher management positions should prove their skills at marketing and negotiation.

- Trade secrets should be carefully guarded from competitors. At the same time, employees are encouraged to find out as much as they can about competitors' plans at trade association meetings and through contacts with customers.

These values are influential in shaping the organizational culture at Prime Pet Foods. The emphasis on the customer has accorded the marketing research department high status, and that department's studies strongly determine product design criteria and promotion policies. The concern with cost control has led to a strongly hierarchical management structure with formal review procedures and detailed policy guidelines. Although suggestions for improvement are encouraged and managers pride themselves in being open to new ideas, significant hurdles must be overcome before such ideas are accepted and implemented. Supermarket buyers are pampered when they visit the company's facilities, and management is generous with expense accounts to entertain them. Hardworking and loyal employees are valued and rewarded, but the division is quick to terminate those who make mistakes or who perform poorly. Virtually all top managers have marketing backgrounds and tend to be impatient with production or research people who cannot respond to market changes on short notice. Quality control is viewed as a necessary evil. As one manager puts it, "After all, dogs don't complain."

As this review suggests, Prime Pet Foods has a particular way of doing business that makes some visions less likely to be successful without major changes. For example, Prime's orientation toward supermarket distribution would make it difficult to shift to marketing through veterinarians or pet stores. On the other hand, a new line of dog snacks or treats would fit the culture very well. But even this conclusion would depend on other self-perceived strengths and weaknesses.

2. *What are the operating strengths and weaknesses of the organization?*

A new vision is easiest to implement if it builds on the organization's existing strengths and avoids its weaknesses. For example, when IBM decided to enter the personal computer business, it knew that it already had the industry's strongest marketing and technical skills. On the other hand, AT&T's foray into the same business was a failure because, although it did have technical and manufacturing skills, its competitive marketing capabilities after years as a regulated monopoly were simply not up to the challenge.

Ten of the most important strengths and weaknesses of Prime Pet Foods are summarized in Table 3.1. Some hints about a new vision become apparent. For example, the declining market share and limited product line point to the need for additional product innovation.

3. *What is the current strategy, and can it be defended?*

A strategy is "the pattern or plan that integrates an organization's major goals, policies, and action sequence into a cohesive whole" (Quinn, Mintzberg, and James, 1988, p. 3). Whether articulated or not, every organization has a strategy that encapsulates the major decisions and commitments of top management on how to position the organization in its environment. Strategic management is a well-established discipline (see, for example, Rowe, Mason, Dickel, and Snyder, 1989; Quinn, Mintzberg, and James, 1988; Thompson and Strickland, 1990; Hill and Jones, 1989), and many organizations go to great lengths to develop and document such strategies. Where a strategy is not formally articulated, it often can be inferred from decisions about resource allocation or from the major actions of the organization.

**Table 3.1. Strengths and Weaknesses of Prime Pet Foods.**

| Strengths | Weaknesses |
|---|---|
| 1. Dependable financial backing from powerful parent company | 1. Parent company slow to authorize new strategic investments |
| 2. Well-established brand names in U.S. markets | 2. Large, well-entrenched competitors |
| 3. Good profit margins | 3. Declining market share |
| 4. Reputation for good value | 4. Limited product line |
| 5. Excellent marketing research department | 5. Risk-averse management |
| 6. Low-cost production plant | 6. Inflexible manufacturing |
| 7. Location close to key suppliers | 7. High cost of transporting products to markets |
| 8. High worker productivity | 8. Excessive inventory costs |
| 9. Good technical staff with access to parent company's strong research skills | 9. Less innovative and slower to respond to changing market conditions than competitors |
| 10. Loyal, well-trained work force | 10. Sporadic breakdowns in top-down communications |

It is useful to examine the current strategy because of what it may suggest about the underlying vision. Sometimes the vision is not clearly stated but can be inferred from the strategy. For example, a city's master plan for zoning, which is a form of strategy, says much about the city's aspirations, the direction in which it intends to grow, and what it hopes to become. Even in the absence of a well-formulated master plan, however, zoning decisions made over time form the pattern of a de facto strategy, and that pattern may contain hints of an underlying vision.

In the case of Prime Pet Foods, the strategy is to attain a competitive advantage in the United States by being the low-cost producer of dog and cat foods and by aggressively advertising its own brand names. The strategy implies a vision of a company dominating a large sector — that is, the low-cost food sector — of the growing pet food market. That vision is undermined by these facts: the company is losing overall market share in the pet food business and the low-priced food sector is not growing as fast as some other parts of the industry, notably gourmet and frozen foods.

Thus far, we have explored the fundamental nature of the organization and how it operates. Now, we need to understand where it appears to be headed if it keeps on its current path.

## THE VISION AUDIT

Many organizations are driven by visions of a more desirable future, but even if no vision has ever been consciously stated, every organization has its own momentum. An organization may move slowly, like a venerable art museum, or more quickly, like a high-growth computer software company; but it does move, and if we chart that movement, we get a sense of where the organization may end up in the future if it keeps going as it is.

This is not a frivolous exercise. For example, economists who plotted the direction of U.S. television, consumer electronics, and automobile businesses over the last decade warned that the United States appeared to be in decline with respect to these industries. Now economists are warning that the United States may be losing its technological edge in other key industries of the twenty-first century. The alarm has been raised. If they choose to do so, government and corporate leaders can formulate new visions and take actions to reverse these trends.

The best way to gauge momentum is to do what I call a vision audit. The questions to be answered in such an audit are the following:

1. Does the organization have a clearly stated vision? If so, what is it?

**2.** If the organization continues on its current path, where will it be heading over the next decade? How good would such a direction be?

**3.** Do the key people in the organization know where the organization is headed and agree on the direction?

**4.** Do the structures, processes, personnel, incentives, and information systems support the current direction of the organization?

These questions are answered below for Prime Pet Foods.

*1. Does the organization have a clearly stated vision? If so, what is it?*

Few organizations have a clearly stated vision. Although many top executives think their vision is clearly stated, upon closer examination it is apparent they are referring to a mission statement or a published credo or even to an advertising slogan. Prime Pet Foods does have what it calls a vision. According to the president of the division, Prime hopes within a decade to be the largest supplier of dog and cat foods in North America. By this point, you should be well aware of the inadequacy of this type of vision statement.

*2. If the organization continues on its current path, where will it be heading over the next decade? How good would such a direction be?*

Leaders have a tendency to be overly optimistic about the future prospects of their organizations. After all, they would not be in leadership roles unless they had confidence in themselves and in their ability to make the organization successful. Still, at this point, they must make a cold, hard, and brutally realistic appraisal of future prospects. Discussions with knowledgeable outsiders like consultants, customers, or stock market analysts may provide a sobering reality test of their perceptions.

In the case of Prime Pet Foods, the prognosis is not especially good. The good news is that pet ownership is increasing, albeit slowly. However, the division is already losing market share in the pet food industry, and its products are in the lower-growth portions of the market. It has formidable competitors who are financially strong and innovative. If the company continues as it has in the past decade, the most likely results are a smaller overall market share (even if Prime dominates the low-cost pet food market), stagnant or slowly growing sales, and a gradual erosion of current cost advantages as others bring more modern plants on line and improve economies of scale. Thus, the inconsistency between Prime's vision and reality seems to require at least a modification of their current sense of direction and, more likely, a whole new vision.

### 3. Do the key people in the organization know where the organization is headed and agree on the direction?

For a vision to be effective, it must be well understood and widely shared in the organization. Leaders often are amazed to learn that although they are quite sure of their sense of direction, the message hasn't reached lower levels in the organization. Perhaps the vision was not as clear as it should have been in the first place, or it was distorted in delivery. A common symptom of poor communication of vision is an overactive rumor mill, as workers grope for scraps of information about where the organization is really headed.

In Prime Pet Foods there is widespread understanding of financial goals and no ambiguity about the cost containment strategy that has affected most managers. However, there is no shared sense of direction. This conclusion is supported by comments from lower-level managers who express confusion about Prime's vision. Many think the parent company wants them to diversify into other product lines using their well-established brand names. Some think the company should acquire a frozen-food manufacturer to get a foothold in the fastest-growing segment of the pet food market. Others fear they may some day lose their autonomy by being merged with other businesses of the parent company.

## 4.  Do the structures, processes, personnel, incentives, and information systems support the current direction of the organization?

Once a vision exists, it can succeed only if the organization is positioned to support it. Prime Pet Foods presents a mixed picture in this regard. For example, with an emphasis on cost efficiency, the division has tight cost control systems with elaborate sign-off procedures. However, this often limits the sales department's ability to respond quickly to marketing opportunities and has caused problems in worker morale when simple requests requiring small amounts of money are delayed or denied even if they will save money in the long run. Similarly, while the information systems governing production and inventories are excellent, the sales department claims that more information on customers would help increase sales. The incentive systems do support the vision in that sales personnel get bonuses when they exceed quotas and factory managers get raises based partly on cost reductions, but all the incentive systems reward short-term behavior and don't encourage managers to do things that will have longer-range payoffs. Thus, while some of the operating practices support the stated vision, others do not, which raises questions about how committed leadership and management are to the vision.

To summarize, a dozen questions were asked about current organizational directions. They highlight the most important factors bearing on an organization's current status and direction. We looked at a consumer products company (Prime Pet Foods) as an example, but these questions should apply equally well to your own organization, no matter what business or field you are in. The Appendix to this book illustrates how these questions might be answered for a totally different type of organization—a government agency.

Having established a baseline and determined whether you need a new vision for your organization, you are now ready to begin to design one. As the architect of your organization's future, you should begin to think like an architect. What has to be satisfied by the new vision? What does a successful design have to accomplish? How should its scope be bounded? These are the concerns we now address.

# CHAPTER 4

# Testing Reality:
## The Vision Scope

O body swayed to music. O brightening glance,
How can we know the dancer from the dance?
—WILLIAM BUTLER YEATS

Leaders, like artists, attempt to create extraordinary new realities out of ordinary materials through the force of vision. The choreographer has dancers and a stage; the painter has a canvas, brushes, and colors; the composer has musicians and instruments; but the only dance, painting, or composition that is noteworthy and successful is one that is informed by an exceptional vision. Just so, the leader creates an enduring institution out of ordinary resources—human, physical, and financial—through a unifying and compelling vision, for leadership, too, is an art form.

This metaphor can be taken one step further. The choreographer, painter, and composer can think great thoughts and have great visions—enobling, uplifting, pathbreaking—and yet the manifestation of their inspiration is expressed within clear boundaries. In the end, the choreographer has human movement to communicate a vision; the painter is constrained by what can be expressed on a two-dimensional surface; and the composer makes sounds within a limited repertoire of notes and instruments. These boundaries do not necessarily limit the artist's vision of what is desirable but rather define the scope of what is achievable, thus providing an indispensable reality test on the vision.

The scope of your vision must be similarly defined and reality tested. For an organization, the scope is defined first by considering the needs of those who have important stakes in the organization and then by examining a variety of other factors, including time, space, and purpose. This chapter will help you understand the necessary scope of your new vision.

# CONSTITUENCIES AND THEIR NEEDS

Every organization has major constituencies or stakeholders, whose needs are ignored at the organization's peril. Bankruptcy courts are littered with examples: the savings and loan institutions whose high-risk real estate loans ignored the need of their depositors for safety of capital; the asbestos manufacturing firms that ignored the exposure of their employees to unsafe working conditions; the chemical companies that ignored the demands of local communities for unpolluted air and water.

A stakeholder is anyone who has the power to exert an influence on your organization or who is strongly influenced by your organization in some significant way. A stakeholder may be a single person, a group of individuals, or another large organization or institution. Each has a unique involvement with your organization and differing interests, priorities, and expectations. To understand the role of stakeholders in your vision, you need to answer these four questions:

1. Who are the most critical stakeholders—both inside and outside your organization—and of these, which are the most important?

2.   What are the major interests and expectations of the five or six most important stakeholders regarding the future of your organization?

3.   What threats or opportunities emanate from these critical stakeholders?

4.   Considering yourself a stakeholder, what do you personally and passionately want to make happen in your organization?

These questions are answered below in the context of Prime Pet Foods.

### 1.   *Who are the most critical stakeholders—both inside and outside your organization—and of these, which are the most important?*

Every organization has many stakeholders, so the first task is simply to list them all. For most organizations, such a list would include at least the major customers or users of the organization's products or services, employees, owners, major competitors, key suppliers, lenders, and the communities within which they operate. After you list all the stakeholders in your organization, pick the five or six most important ones—that is, those with the most interest in or impact on the future of your organization.

In the case of Prime Pet Foods, the stakeholder list includes the following:

- Supermarkets
- Pet owners
- The parent company
- Workers
- Managers
- Competitors

- Veterinarians

- Suppliers

- Regulators in federal and state governments

- Consumerists

- The media

- The research community

- Shippers and handlers

All of these stakeholders are important to the company. For example, veterinarians often influence pet owners in the choice of pet foods by their recommendations regarding nutrition, and regulators have a strong interest in product safety, labeling, advertising claims, and pollution control. Still, on reviewing the list, the leaders of Prime Pet Foods might pick the first six stakeholders as having the most influence on the future directions of the division.

**2.** *What are the major interests and expectations of the five or six most important stakeholders regarding the future of your organization?*

Each stakeholder group has its own needs and expectations regarding your organization—and some power to influence your choice of vision. Some of your stakeholders may be highly dependent on your organization to supply certain kinds of products or services. Others may expect only a minimum level of responsible behavior. By virtue of being important stakeholders, however, all of them have some power to react negatively, perhaps even forcefully, if your organization disappoints them. Thus, you'd like your new vision to be as accommodating of them as possible.

The Prime Pet Foods division might list the needs and expectations of its top six stakeholders as follows:

Supermarkets

- High-volume demand for Prime's products
- Good profit margins for the market
- Dependable supply
- Satisfied repeat customers
- Safe and high-quality products
- Product diversity and innovation
- Well-advertised and promoted products
- Easy logistics (handling, shelf space, damage resistance)

Pet Owners

- High-quality pet foods at a reasonable price
- Acceptance by pets (palatability, variety)
- Safe and nutritious foods
- Product convenience and storage stability
- Hygienic and neat usage
- Products appropriate to pets' age, role
- Informative and honest advertising and labeling

Prime's Parent Company

- Adequate return on investment
- High ethical standards/freedom from legal entanglements
- Customer satisfaction and strong brand loyalty
- Growth opportunities

- Image/pride/public approval
- Low financial risk

Workers

- Job security
- Good/safe working conditions
- Competitive wages and benefits
- Job satisfaction
- Image/pride/public approval of company
- Opportunities for personal growth

Managers

- Growth and profitability
- Customer satisfaction
- Image/pride/reputation in industry
- Freedom from legal or parent company hassles
- Product diversity and innovation
- Opportunities for personal/professional growth

Competitors

- Ethical behavior in the marketplace
- Active support of and participation in the industry's trade association and lobbying efforts
- Nutritious and safe products to avoid industry hassles from regulators and consumerists

Not surprisingly, some needs and expectations are widely shared among major stakeholders (for example, growth and profitability, desire for pride and public approval, customer satisfaction, product quality, safety and innovation), and these should command the most attention when you are contemplating a potential new vision.

### 3. *What threats or opportunities emanate from these critical stakeholders?*

Since, by definition, each stakeholder has some influence over your organization, it follows that each may offer new opportunities or pose future threats, and you must clearly understand these as you formulate your vision.

The *supermarket chains,* for example, might provide additional shelf space for Prime's pet food products and perhaps for some non–pet food products that share the brand name and promotional efforts of the company. Supermarkets might also help by providing market research information or featuring Prime's products in their own advertising. On the other hand, Prime is vulnerable to the threat that supermarkets might give it less shelf space in the future, especially if the total pet food market declines or a competitor comes out with faster-selling or higher-margin products.

*Pet owners* offer many opportunities and threats to Prime. If dog and cat ownership increases, the total pet food market will increase. The desire of pet owners for greater convenience and variety in pet foods creates new product and packaging opportunities. Increased concern for the pet's health, grooming, and recreational needs may offer new product opportunities complementary to food items. On the other hand, Prime is vulnerable if pet ownership decreases or begins to favor smaller animals, both possibilities that would decrease total food sales. Another threat is that Prime's products will come to be seen by pet owners as old-fashioned, too expensive, or not as attractive as those of more innovative competitors. Perhaps the most serious threat would arise if some animals became sick or died as a result of Prime's products. Such a scenario would require the company to defend itself against consumerist accusations, bad publicity, and possible lawsuits.

The *parent company* offers Prime strong financial support, especially for well-conceived investment programs, a strong international marketing presence that can be tapped for new product ideas or potential foreign expansion, and an excellent research and new product development staff. However, the parent company also poses a threat in that it may seek greater control over Prime's operations, may split off or sell the division at any time, or may treat Prime as a cash cow, expecting strong contributions to overall earnings but refusing to reinvest profits in future expansion of the division.

The *workers* at Prime Pet Foods can be a continuing source of new ideas for product, marketing, and production process improvements. They can also help to lower wastage, raise product quality and safety, and learn new skills that can be employed to the company's benefit. Workers can also pose threats to Prime's future, including resistance to needed automation, excessive demands for wages and benefits—perhaps backed up by the threat of strikes—or refusal to adapt to new work procedures.

Prime Pet Food's *managers* are a talented, competitive, and experienced group of individuals who offer many opportunities for company growth. They are experts in consumer marketing, have excellent contacts in the trade (especially with supermarket chains), and are skillful in all aspects of food production and distribution operations. The main threat from the management group is turnover of key personnel, a constant concern in a highly competitive industry. In fact, a few managers left or retired soon after the acquisition by the parent company, and several others expect to be asked by the parent company to transfer to positions in other divisions. There are also some managers who are resistant to change.

There are strong *competitors* in this industry that can be expected to do everything they can to steal market share from Prime Pet Foods. The only opportunity they offer is the possible acquisition of some of the smaller pet food companies with interesting niches in the market. Beyond this, competitors pose many threats, including the possibility of destructive price wars, aggressive bidding to obtain supermarket shelf space currently used by Prime, innovative new products, or clever, heavily supported advertising campaigns aimed at capturing Prime's market share.

These opportunities and threats suggest that Prime's market share in the pet food business is vulnerable and needs to be strongly defended just to hold steady. As noted in Chapter Three, Prime's market share is already slipping, and the entire pet food market is growing at less than 4 percent per year. These figures reinforce the need for a new direction if the division's sales are to increase significantly in the future.

### 4. *Considering yourself a stakeholder, what do you personally and passionately want to make happen in your organization?*

As leader of your organization, you are also a major stakeholder. As such, your own needs, desires, drives, and aspirations must play a key role in the vision formation process. It is vital that you be completely honest with yourself and quite clear about what you want to get out of your organization, as well as the nature of the legacy you wish to leave when your tenure as leader is over.

The president of Prime Pet Foods might say that he wants to leave an organization that has grown significantly in revenues and earnings, has attained a reputation as an industry leader in product quality and safety, and is highly respected for its contributions to the health, happiness, and life-styles of pet owners and pets. He might also say that he wants to create an environment in the company that is challenging and enjoyable for himself and for other employees, especially one that maximizes his own freedom to operate with minimum interference from the parent company. If he were young enough to contemplate one or more promotions, he might also admit he is striving to demonstrate through his leadership at Prime that he can build the kind of competitively aggressive, yet highly ethical, organization that would qualify him for increased responsibilities at higher levels in the parent company or elsewhere.

The analysis of your organization's stakeholders should provide some clues to possible visions for the future. At this point, for example, we are beginning to suspect that Prime Pet Foods might require a new thrust (possibly not even in the pet food business) that would take advantage of the division's strengths and its position among key stakeholders. The next task is to target the vision more clearly.

# TARGETING YOUR VISION

When Frances Hesselbein took over as executive director of the Girl Scouts of the U.S.A. in 1976, she was faced with many troubles. The institution seemed tired and out of step with the world around it. Teenage girls were losing interest in becoming members, volunteers were getting hard to find, the Boy Scouts were threatening to extend membership to girls, and women's rights groups wanted to convert the organization into a boot camp for political and social activists. Hesselbein realized that, above all, the Girl Scouts needed a renewed sense of direction and commitment. But where to begin?

Hesselbein needed to make some key decisions to help her find the right direction. What would the vision have to accomplish? What critical issues would need to be addressed? Were there any limits—social, political, geographical, and so forth—that should shape her thinking?

She confronted these questions deliberately and systematically and then went on to develop a concept for the future of the Girl Scouts that stands today as a monument to leadership of a nonprofit organization. "We are really here for one reason," she told a reporter, "to help a girl reach her highest potential. More than any one thing, that made the difference" (Byrne, 1990, p. 72). From there, it was a short step to realizing that Girl Scouts had to reach out to all girls, especially minorities, had to provide experiences relevant to the emerging realities of women in the modern world (in such areas as technology, careers, and environmental concerns), and had to develop a whole new organizational concept to tap the creativity and initiative of volunteers.

As you think about the new vision for your organization, consider how the vision should be bounded by asking these questions:

1. What are the boundaries to your new vision? For example, are there time, geographical, or social constraints?

2. What must the vision accomplish? How will you know when it is successful?

3. Which critical issues must be addressed in the vision?

To illustrate, Prime's leaders might answer these questions as follows:

*1.   What are the boundaries to your new vision? For example, are there time, geographical, or social constraints?*
A vision should have the clarity and focus to communicate precisely what direction is intended. At this stage in the vision-forming process, you need to begin to specify what will be contained in the vision and what will not.

How far ahead should your vision focus? That depends on the time it takes to put major changes in place. For a consumer products firm in a fast-moving industry like fashions or electronics, five to seven years may be just right, while for an electric utility with long lead times for adding capacity, ten to fifteen years may be more appropriate.

What about other boundaries? A small restaurant chain may need to limit its vision to a geographical region defined by the reach of a few metropolitan newspapers in order to maximize the impact of its advertising dollar. A museum may be limited by economic realities and donor restrictions to certain periods or types of art. For the Girl Scouts, Francis Hesselbein's vision was designed for all American girls, but by choice it excluded close ties to groups with different agendas, like women's rights associations.

In the case of Prime Pet Foods, seven years might be a reasonable stretch for a vision, far enough ahead to contemplate a real change in direction but still within a time span meaningful for the careers of the current leadership. By a decision of its parent company, Prime's marketing is limited to the United States and Canada. Since the parent company has other subsidiaries in the food business in the United States, Prime is also limited to animal foods. However, it could consider foods for animals other than dogs and cats, for example, birds, reptiles, hamsters, or even livestock. Similarly Prime is free to consider nonfood products or services for pets, especially those that would take advantage of Prime's excellent brand name and distribution system.

## 2. What must the vision accomplish? How will you know when it is successful?

Shortly after Douglas Wilder took office as the first black governor of Virginia on January 13, 1990, he told a reporter who asked him about his aspirations, "I've always believed in the art of the possible. I believe there's a difference between brave-heartedness and foolishness and I believe in whatever I'm going to do, if I don't see success somewhere through the tunnel of that vision, I don't even bother with it" (Abrams, 1990, p. E1).

A clear distinction should be made between the vision itself, which is a substantive statement of intent or direction, and the measures of success of that vision. Many people tend to confuse the two. For example, the leader of an advertising agency may have a vision of her agency as the preeminent expert in media advertising for the men's fashion industry worldwide. That statement meets the test of vision as described in Chapter Two in that it serves to inform and inspire others, to clarify purpose and direction, to reflect the uniqueness of the organization, and to serve as a guide to strategy and action. On the other hand, if the leader said she wanted her agency to quadruple its bookings in five years, this statement is not a vision because it fails those tests. Nonetheless, one of the reasons she chose the vision statement in the first place might have been a desire to make her agency grow substantially, and if the vision is realistic and works as intended, bookings may very well quadruple as a result. Thus, measures of success help the leader understand what kind of vision is needed, even though they must never be confused with the vision itself.

Of course, measures of success should go well beyond profit statements or growth aspirations. For the Girl Scouts, the vision would not have been successful if it had not increased the quality and quantity of volunteers, so critical to the organization. It also needed to make the organization more attractive to girls and their parents so they would be proud to join, needed to increase the stature and reputation of the organization, and so forth. Knowing what it takes for a vision to be successful contributes significantly to the scoping decision.

In the case of Prime Pet Foods, a number of possible measures of success for the vision come to mind, including the following:

Growth Measures

- Sales growth

- Profitability

- Market share

- Return on investment

Cost Reduction Measures

- Raw materials costs

- Processing costs

- Transportation costs

- Marketing and distribution costs

Measures of Satisfaction of Ethical/Legal Obligations

- Environmental protection
- Food purity and nutrition
- Honesty in food labeling and advertising
- Integrity
- Number of lawsuits
- Workplace safety

Innovation Measures

- New product development and introduction
- Number of patents
- Improved production or distribution processes
- Number of new suggestions received
- Product diversity

Image Measures

- Degree of customer satisfaction
- Number of returns and complaints
- Reputation for product quality and value

Management and Worker Performance Measures

- Number and quality of managers and workers
- Productivity of workers
- Turnover and absenteeism
- Training and skills enhancement
- Flexibility of the work force

- Quality of managerial decision making
- Growth in promotional opportunities

After writing down all the possible measures of success for your vision statement, you will probably find the list too long. As a practical matter, it is best to concentrate on no more than five to seven of the most important of these measures.

The president of Prime Pet Foods might review the foregoing list and reason as follows:

- Some reasonable degree of growth is surely necessary if we are to remain in good favor with our parent company, continuing to receive their financial support and retaining our operating freedom (which means a lot to me). Besides, the managers need growth to ensure promotional opportunities for them in the future, and if we don't grow, we won't be able to keep up with the competitors, who are increasing their attacks on our market share with their heavy promotions and successful new products. Therefore, any new vision certainly needs to enable our sales and profits to grow at least at the rate of the overall parent company average, about 12 percent per year.

- Since total industry sales are growing at only 4 percent per year, we'll have to do something rather dramatic to reach those 12 percent targets. Clearly, whatever new vision we develop must either stimulate innovation in our existing product lines or, more likely, lead to whole new product lines outside our traditional pet food business. Tentatively, let's think of a new direction that would ensure that at least 50 percent of our sales in seven years consists of new products or services not part of our current business mix. Moreover, to reduce our vulnerability to loss of market share, let's seek to expand our product diversity so that no single product line accounts for more than 20 percent of the business.

- Customer satisfaction, especially in the form of repeat customers, is the key to growth in the consumer products industry no matter what we produce. To promote this, we must strive for the very highest product quality and value possible.

The net result of this line of reasoning is a narrowing down of the measures of success for Prime Pet Food's vision to six key measures: sales growth, profits growth, innovation, product diversity, customer satisfaction, and high product quality and value.

**3.   Which critical issues must be addressed in the vision?**
Inherent in every organization are certain fundamental issues that may be resolvable through a new vision. For example, a fundamental issue for the Girl Scouts was relevance: how could the organization make its programs relevant to the emerging real world context for young girls? The reality is that independent careers will be far more important to women in the future, with homemaker skills less so. What could the Girl Scouts do to provide the skills, attitudes, and values to help young girls prepare for their future world of work? As a visionary leader you must be aware of these kinds of fundamental issues and be alert to their implications for your new vision statement.

In the Prime Pet Foods example, there are several fundamental issues confronting the industry today. One issue concerns the changing nature of pet ownership. Although overall pet ownership is increasing, the mix of pets is changing. As a result of fewer families living in detached homes and having time available for exercising pets, the cat population grew 44 percent (to 63 million) from 1982 to 1990, while the dog population grew only 13 percent (to 54.5 million) in the same time period (*Pet Food Institute Fact Sheet, 1990, 1991*). Since a cat consumes less pet food than the average dog and since the size of the average dog has also been decreasing, a relatively stable or perhaps even declining total pet food market is likely in the next decade. The issue this poses for the industry is that regardless of the market appeal of innovative new pet food products, fundamental demand cannot be increased much unless pet ownership can be increased beyond historic rates. Thus, any onc company's growth is likely to be at the expense of a competitor's market share, so here again, the implication for Prime's pet food business is that Prime has to look elsewhere if it wishes to find growth opportunities.

Another fundamental issue facing the pet food business is consumerist and regulatory interest in pet food safety, nutrition, truth in labeling and advertising, and pollution control. Although pet food manufacturers have better rccords in these regards than some other industries, the very size of the industry, the care and affection that people lavish on their pets, and the vulnerability of pets themselves combine to make the industry a closely watched one. Clearly, whatever vision Prime chooses should be sensitive to this issue.

At this point, you should have developed a pretty good idea what you want your new vision to accomplish. You have considered your own needs and those of the most important stakeholders in your organization. You have also decided on the scope of your vision—its time horizon, what it must accomplish, and which key issues it should address.

Since all visions must deal with the future, you should now be ready to think about how the future is likely to develop for your organization and where your vision fits into it.

# CHAPTER 5

# Considering the Possibilities:
## The Vision Context

Time past and time future
　　What might have been and what has been
　　Point to one end, which is always
　　present . . .
The detail of the pattern is movement.
　　—T. S. ELIOT

Here's a riddle: can you remember the year when the average starting salary of a teacher in the United States was only $8,200 per year, the median sales price of a new home was under $40,000, a 10¢ stamp carried your first-class letter from New York to Los Angeles, the average car got 13.5 miles per gallon, and only a handful of computer wizards could even remotely conceive of the possibility of a desktop computer?

For the college students I teach this sounds like ancient history, a time out of the distant past so remote as to be totally irrelevant to the daily realities they face, much less the job market they will shortly be entering. Their parents have much less of a problem remembering the year in question, but my students consider it preposterous when I tell them they will need to think as far ahead as the riddle goes back in time if they are to formulate realistic visions for their organizations. They shouldn't, for no matter how far out a new vision extends, it is often necessary to look at the full dimensions of the organization's environments at least five to ten years beyond that time to establish that the correct direction has been chosen.

Have you figured it out yet? The year was 1975, not even twenty years ago and well within the memory of just about any college graduate. Chances are, you thought it was much earlier, but we have been experiencing so rapid a rate of change that even a fairly recent time seems more remote than it really is. It works the same way in the opposite direction as well.

Suppose your new vision has a seven-year time horizon. You start right now making the necessary long-term investments and taking the appropriate actions to make your vision a reality. Assume you are successful in realizing the vision at the end of seven years' time. At that point, you hope the organization is well positioned for the following decade — that is, out to the seventeenth year — because that's when you'll be getting the returns on the investments you made. Moreover, being a realist, you know that further changes in direction are likely as the world changes, and your organization must be viable while they are in process, too.

So you need to be able to think a decade or two into the future if you are to form an appropriate vision. But can one think about the future that far ahead with any degree of confidence? Doesn't the riddle prove there can be enormous and probably unforeseeable changes over that time period? To answer these questions, we need a brief excursion.

# HOW TO THINK
# ABOUT THE FUTURE

In Chapter One, we defined a vision as "a realistic, credible, attractive future for your organization." Note that a vision is a choice of one particular future out of the many futures possible for the organization. An imaginative person or group could invent hundreds or perhaps thousands of possible futures for your organization. Many of these would be undesirable, of course, and even some of the desirable ones would prove impractical or be rejected for other reasons. In any event, it is the leader's job to invent—or stimulate others to invent—a range of alternative visions from which the most desirable can be chosen.

You cannot decide about a realistic or desirable future for your organization without reflecting on what might happen in the world that could affect your organization in the future—that is, the totality of the organization's external environment. This includes the future of all the key stakeholders as well as relevant aspects of the social, political, economic, technological, and institutional environments. For example, if you were choosing a vision for General Motors, your vision might well be shaped by expected changes in gasoline prices, consumer preferences, pollution control regulations, electric battery technology, urban commuting patterns, and a broad array of other considerations in the firm's external environments.

Since these external factors are not under your control, they cannot be invented as the vision can. But they still need to be anticipated, studied, and evaluated for their implications for your vision. This is a daunting task, for you know there are many external environments important for your vision, each having many relevant dimensions and each dimension—say, gasoline prices—having many possible futures. How can you be expected to predict all of these with any degree of accuracy?

Obviously, you can't, for no one has the ability to predict the future, notwithstanding all the claims of fortune tellers, astrologers, and other charlatans. The future is inherently uncertain, and the further into the future you attempt to predict, the greater the uncertainty. The uncertainty also increases with the complexity of the area being examined and with the extent to which actual outcomes depend on human actions as opposed to physical or natural ones. Moreover, there will always be surprises in the future since, by definition, a surprise is something that you didn't expect to happen or that completely escaped your attention, and there will always be such occurrences.

Fortunately, you don't have to predict the future in order to develop your vision. Instead, you only need to develop a reasonable understanding of the range and nature of possible outcomes. By doing so, you get three benefits. First, and perhaps most important, thinking about the nature of possible developments in the external environment stimulates your thinking about opportunities for your own organization, thereby contributing directly to the design of your own vision. A study of twenty presidents of successful colleges found that "the opportunity-conscious president has a general concept of how his or her institution must change to be able to respond to inevitable environmental evolution. Such a president will try to position his or her institution to take advantage of future opportunities. . . . They open the door before the knock is heard" (Watkins, 1986, p. 20).

Second, examining possible outcomes helps to ensure that your resulting vision is "robust," that is, likely to be effective in a wide range of possible external conditions. An example of a robust vision was Martin Luther King's vision of racial equality in the United States; it was appropriate and necessary within a wide range of economic and political futures and endures as a motivating vision to this day.

Finally, by looking out a decade beyond the time horizon of your vision, you reduce the likelihood of unpleasant surprises, such as attaining your vision and then finding, as Warner Communications did with the video game business, that it is no longer suitable under unfolding conditions. Instead, with the early warning you get by thinking that far ahead, you'll be in a much better position to build flexibility and a quick response capability into what you envision for your organization.

Thus, you need to think about a range of possible futures in a systematic and productive way without trying to predict what actually will happen. An easy way to do this is outlined below and illustrated in the remaining sections of this chapter:

1.  Identify all the categories of future developments in the external environment that are likely to influence your vision statement.

2.  In each category, draw up a list of your expectations for about ten years beyond the expected duration of your vision statement.

3.  Evaluate the list of expectations to determine which ones would have the greatest impact if they occurred, that is, those that have the greatest significance for your vision statement. For each of these, assign a probability of occurrence based on your best understanding of the item in question.

4.  Write three or four brief scenarios that encompass the range of possible futures you anticipate. List the major implications of each scenario for your vision statement.

You don't have to do this alone, of course. I have had some success in drawing together groups of one or two dozen knowledgeable people in an organization and doing this as a team project over a couple of days (Nanus, 1982). Parts of the task can be delegated to a committee. You can also simply ask people whose opinions you respect to send you notes on what they see as the critical determinants of your organization's future.

In following these steps, you create your own mental model of how the world is likely to evolve and what your organization must do to be successful. So now, let's see how this process might work with the Prime Pet Foods example.

# IDENTIFYING IMPORTANT FUTURE DEVELOPMENTS

Thinking about the future can be fun. As a student once said to me, "I like thinking about the future, because that's where I expect to live the rest of my life." It happens that we're all pretty good at it, too. In fact, several scholars have remarked that the ability to think about the future is a distinctly human quality that sets us apart from all other species. This ability enables us to act not just in response to an actual physical stimulus, as all other animals do, but also to images of future worlds that exist only in the mind.

To start thinking about the future, identify all the categories of relevant developments. For most organizations, these include future changes in the needs and wants served by the organization, in the major stakeholders, and in the economic, social, political, and technological environments. An additional category of "other" is usually sufficient to catch anything else of importance.

The next step is to examine each category in turn and list changes that could make a difference to the organization. It is helpful in drawing up this list to recognize that the future is composed of three parts: continuity, change, and choice. Continuity arises from the tendency of all institutions and many data series to have a certain amount of inertia and momentum. For example, demographic trends can often be projected with some confidence into the future, as can certain enduring structures such as the U.S. legal system. Change refers to developments that could occur when limits to existing trends are reached or from one-time events that alter existing assumptions. An example of the former would be a reversal of the trend toward increasing urban air pollution after some totally unacceptable threshold is reached; an example of the latter is a technological breakthrough. Choice simply refers to major developments that result from human actions, such as the decision of Saddam Hussein to attack Kuwait or the subsequent decision of President Bush to oppose him with military force.

In thinking about future developments, it may be helpful to become familiar with some of the forecasts of professional futurists, people who earn their living studying likely future trends and developments. You can learn about such forecasts by writing to the World Future Society (4916 St. Elmo Avenue, Bethesda, Md., 20814) or referring to some recent books (for example, see Drucker, 1989; Coates, 1989; Naisbitt and Aburdene, 1990; Brown and others, 1992; Davis and Davidson, 1991; Schwartz, 1991).

The list that follows presents some key questions regarding future developments:

1. What major changes can be expected in the needs and wants served by your organization in the future?

2. What changes can be expected in the major stakeholders of your organization in the future?

3. What major changes can be expected in the relevant economic environments in the future?

4. What major changes can be expected in the relevant social environments in the future?

5. What major changes can be expected in the relevant political environments in the future?

6. What major changes can be expected in the relevant technological environments in the future?

7. What major changes can be expected in other external environments that could affect your organization in the future?

These questions are answered below using Prime Pet Foods. The answers are for illustrative purposes only; in most real situations, including yours, the lists would undoubtedly be much longer. Remember also that these are significant possible developments, not necessarily probable ones, as the probability assessment occurs independently in the next section. In other words, you are not saying they are likely, only that they are possible and would affect your vision in some significant way if they occurred.

*1.   What major changes can be expected in the needs and wants served by your organization in the future ?*

Every organization provides some sort of service to people or other organizations. These outsiders may be called customers, clients, or a variety of other titles, such as parishioners for a church, students for a school, or taxpayers for a public agency. Whatever they may be called in your case, they have certain needs and wants that are satisfied by your organization, and it is important that you think about how these needs and wants may change in the future.

In the case of Prime Pet Foods, some of these changes may include the following:

a. Rising population of show animals, such as pedigree dogs, increases demand for special foods and "gourmet" items

b. Breakthrough in pet longevity

c. Increased reliance on veterinarians as source of advice and perhaps as supplier of pet foods

d. Demand for "treats," such as dog biscuits and snacks, increases faster than any other pet food category

e. Increased demand for convenience and self-feeding in pet foods

f. Discovery that pets may be harmful to human health

g. Increased demand for pet foods that more closely resemble human foods

h. More concern with pet health and nutrition, including special diet foods

*2.   What changes can be expected in the major stakeholders of your organization in the future?*

In Chapter Four, you identified the key stakeholders in your organization. Now you need to list possible changes that each stakeholder could initiate that may affect your vision statement. A few examples for Prime Pet Foods include the following:

Supermarkets

a. Increased shelf space for lower-cost but higher-margin house brands to compete with national brands

b. Improved information systems to track brand movement and allocate shelf space

c. Pressure on pet food companies to spend more on advertising and in-store promotion of pet foods

d. Increased stocking of nonfood pet items such as health items, accessories, and grooming supplies

e. Increased store size, with some "hypermarkets" including pet store boutiques

Pet Owners

f. Decline in dog ownership, especially of large dogs, as the baby boom population ages, their children leave home, and they spend less time at home

g. Smaller square footage in family homes, which moves pet ownership toward cats, birds, and small mammals or reptiles

h. Increased anthropomorphism (treating pets like children), which raises demand for pet clothes, toys, accessories, grooming, and so forth

i. More eating out by double-income families, resulting in fewer table scraps that can be used as pet food

j. Great increase in the use of pet-sitting services and kennels to look after pets while owners travel

Parent Company

k.  Decides to exit the pet food business and sell Prime Pet Foods

l.  Merges Prime with its other pet food subsidiaries in other countries to form an international pet food subsidiary, which shares brands and research capabilities

m.  Treats Prime as a cash cow, reducing the portion of cash flow Prime is allowed to retain for investment

n.  Merges Prime with its other U.S. food subsidiaries to leverage parent company clout with supermarkets and advertising media

o.  Adopts Prime's products and brand names for expansion into new overseas markets

Workers

p.  Flextime and/or a four-day work week is extended to Prime's workers

q.  Increased demand for worker entitlements raises benefit costs

r.  Influence of unions in Prime's plants and facilities decreases

s.  Multicultural, multilingual work force

t.  More highly educated work force

Managers

u.  More women managers at higher levels

v.  Fewer layers of management due to automation and powerful information technologies

w. More worker participation in management processes

x. Increased emphasis on mentoring and networking

Competitors

xx. Greater industry concentration, with more national brands and fewer local brands

y. New entries into the pet food business by major consumer firms

yy. New outlets for pet foods, such as pet supply stores in shopping centers or distribution through gas stations

z. Higher costs of new product introduction, including marketing research, market tests, and advertising

zz. Significant new product breakthrough reported by a major competitor

## 3. What major changes can be expected in the relevant economic environments in the future?

It is hard to think of an organization that is not in some way affected by the general health of the economy. To answer this question, you need to identify possible trends and developments in the international, national, and local economies that could affect your vision.

A few examples of economic developments critical to Prime are the following:

a. Higher long-term interest costs make plant and equipment investment more expensive for U.S. firms, thereby increasing the competitive advantage of firms like Prime with direct access to foreign funds

b. A major recession or depression causes a substantial decrease in pet ownership

c. Energy costs increase, raising the cost of food processing and transportation

    d. Food costs at least double in the United States

    e. World famine makes pet ownership in the United States appear to be insensitive, self-indulgent, and wasteful of food needed elsewhere for survival

**4.    What major changes can be expected in the relevant social environments in the future?**
    Social changes include changes in values, tastes, lifestyles, demographics, work, and leisure and in other factors in society that bear on the way your organization operates or on the products and services it supplies. A few examples for Prime Pet Foods are as follows:

    a. Increased prohibition of pets in certain locations, for example, small apartments, condos, some public parks

    b. More people working at home rather than commuting increases the demand for pets to relieve loneliness

    c. Pet companionship found beneficial to health of growing population of older people

    d. Higher crime rates increase use of pets for protection and patrol purposes

    e. Fractionalization of mass advertising audiences due to proliferation of cable television, special interest magazines, and so forth

**5.    What major changes can be expected in the relevant political environments in the future?**
    Hardly any organization is immune to changes in government regulation (at all levels) or to political pressures in areas like environmentalism, consumerism, or civil rights. Some examples relevant to Prime are listed below:

    a. Much more stringent pollution control regulations on dust, noise, odors, and waste disposal

b. Luxury taxes on pet foods or higher licensing fees for pets

c. Tougher standards on pet food quality and nutrition, including tighter regulations on animal by-products, advertising claims, labeling, and the use of chemical additives

d. Increase in class action suits to pursue consumerist and environmentalist agendas

e. New monitoring and records-keeping requirements, especially regarding worker health and safety

**6.   *What major changes can be expected in the relevant technological environments in the future?***

Your organization doesn't have to be in a high technology field to be affected by technological change. Virtually all organizations today use some form of information technology — word processors, cellular phones, facsimile machines, and the like — and most are affected by other technologies as well. You need to think deeply about how vulnerable your vision is to quick and often revolutionary shifts in technology. Here are a few concerns for Prime:

a. Protein analogs substitute for animal by-products in pet foods

b. The tin can is replaced by new packaging alternatives and food preservation methods

c. Foods are designed that contain drugs to control allergies, fleas, and other pet maladies or to alter pet moods

d. A higher level of automation of processing optimizes product yields and increases productivity and quality control

e. A breakthrough occurs in understanding pet nutritional requirements and achieving perfect dietary balance through vitamin and mineral additives

f. Genetic engineering of pets allows some diseases to be eliminated or desirable pet characteristics to be optimized

**7.   *What major changes can be expected in other external environments that could affect your organization in the future?***

There are a wide range of other changes in the outside world that could affect your organization. Your vision might be affected by religious or educational developments, by trends unique to your own industry or professional group, or by the activities of other institutions, such as the media. Here is your chance to identify other key external developments you might have missed using the earlier categories. For example, Prime might need to add the following developments to its list of concerns:

a. Animal by-products for use in pet foods become more expensive as human meat consumption is reduced in response to cholesterol concerns

b. The demand for pet services — including insurance, training, grooming, breeding, pet rentals, and pet shows — expands greatly

c. A national chain of pet supermarkets is franchised, which offers discount prices on pet products, including foods

d. Education about pets becomes a significant market of its own, for example, books, videotapes, audiotapes, classes, computer programs

e. Home breeding of endangered animal species becomes a widespread hobby of environmentally conscious Americans

By now, it should be obvious that many things can happen in the external environments of your organization that could have a direct and meaningful impact on what you can realistically aspire to or achieve. Though by no means complete, the above lists illustrate the wide range of concerns a leader must have even in such a narrowly defined marketplace as pet foods. But generating the lists is only the first step. Now you must put them to use.

# ASSESSING THE SIGNIFICANCE AND PROBABILITIES OF FUTURE DEVELOPMENTS

So far, you have been peering far and wide into the future, hoping not to miss anything that really matters. Perhaps you have generated several hundred items that seem to merit attention. Not all of them are equally important, however, so you need to review the lists carefully to identify those items that will have the greatest impact on your choice of vision.

As a first approximation, review all the items you identified and divide them into four levels of priority based on their impact on your choice of vision. A priority one item would have the greatest impact on your organization's future direction if it were to occur as expected and a priority four item the least impact. If you are working with colleagues, have them do the same, compare the lists, and try to come to some agreement on the priorities. Then look very carefully at the items chosen as priority one items and select a subset of the most critical fifteen to twenty of them for further analysis.

In the case of Prime Pet Foods, the most critical developments chosen from the preceding section are shown in Table 5.1.

You have now listed the most important developments but have not yet decided how likely they are to occur. In order to assign probabilities, you need to restate the items in the

### Table 5.1. Most Critical Future Developments for Prime Pet Foods.

1. More concern with pet health and nutrition, including special diet foods (Item 1h)
2. More shelf space in supermarkets for lower-cost/higher-margin house brands competing with national brands (Item 2a)
3. Increased stocking in supermarkets of nonfood pet items such as health items, accessories, and grooming supplies (Item 2d)
4. Increased store size, with some "hypermarkets" including pet store boutiques (Item 2e)
5. Decline in dog ownership, especially of large dogs, as the baby boom population ages, their children leave home, and they spend less time at home (Item 2f)
6. Smaller square footage in family homes, which moves pet ownership toward cats, birds, and small mammals or reptiles (Item 2g)
7. Increased anthropomorphism (treating pets like children), which increases demand for pet clothes, toys, accessories, grooming, and so forth (Item 2h)
8. Parent company treats Prime as a cash cow, reducing the portion of cash flow Prime is allowed to retain for investment (Item 2m)
9. New entries into the pet food business by major consumer firms (Item 2y)
10. New outlets for pet foods, such as pet supply stores in shopping centers or distribution through gas stations (Item 2yy)
11. Higher costs of new product introduction, including marketing research, market tests, and advertising (Item 2z)
12. Significant new product breakthrough reported by a major competitor (Item 2zz)
13. More people working at home rather than commuting increases the demand for pets to relieve loneliness (Item 4b)
14. Tougher government standards on pet food quality and nutrition, including tighter regulations on animal by-products, advertising claims, labeling, and the use of chemical additives (Item 5c)
15. Increase in class action suits to pursue consumerist and environmentalist agendas (Item 5d)
16. The demand for pet services—including insurance, training, grooming, breeding, pet rentals, and pet shows—expands greatly (Item 7b)
17. Home breeding of endangered animal species becomes a widespread hobby of environmentally conscious Americans (Item 7e)

high-priority list (Table 5.1) unambiguously. Often, the best way to do this is by quantifying the items as much as possible so that you can begin to get a feeling of the magnitudes involved. Then, assign probabilities either qualitatively (for

Table 5.2. Probabilities of Most Critical Future Developments
for Prime Pet Foods.

|  | Probability |
|---|---|
| 1. More concern with pet health and nutrition, leading to at least a tripling in the demand for organic and dietetic pet foods | 90 |
| 2. At least a doubling of shelf space in supermarkets for lower-cost but higher-margin house brands, with commensurate reduction of space for national brands | 40 |
| 3. Nonfood pet items such as health items, accessories, and grooming supplies get at least 30 percent of the total shelf space in supermarkets used for pet products, including food | 70 |
| 4. At least 25 percent of the supermarkets increase their store size, with some "hypermarkets" including pet store boutiques | 20 |
| 5. Dog ownership declines at least 20 percent, especially of large dogs, as the baby boom population ages, their children leave home, and they spend less time at home | 80 |
| 6. Smaller square footage in family homes increases ownership of cats, birds, small mammals, and reptiles by at least 40 percent | 70 |
| 7. Increased anthropomorphism (treating pets like children) at least triples the demand for pet clothes, toys, accessories, grooming, and so forth | 70 |
| 8. Parent company treats Prime as a cash cow, reducing the portion of cash flow Prime is allowed to retain for investment by at least 25 percent | 40 |
| 9. At least two major consumer firms, for example, Procter & Gamble or Heinz, enter the pet food business | 70 |
| 10. New outlets for pet foods, such as pet supply stores in shopping centers or distribution through gas stations, capture at least 20 percent of the national pet food market | 80 |
| 11. New product innovation and introduction costs, including marketing research, market tests, and advertising, at least double | 90 |
| 12. A competitor has a significant new product breakthrough that captures at least a 20 percent share of the pet food market in a five-year period | 30 |
| 13. More people working at home rather than commuting increases the demand for pets to relieve loneliness, raising overall pet ownership by at least 20 percent | 80 |

### Table 5.2. Probabilities of Most Critical Future Developments for Prime Pet Foods, Cont'd.

|  | Probability |
|---|---|
| 14. Tougher government standards on pet food quality and nutrition, including tighter regulations on animal by-products, advertising claims, labeling, and the use of chemical additives, at least double the current cost of compliance for Prime Pet Foods | 90 |
| 15. Class action suits to pursue consumerist and environmentalist agendas at least triple | 60 |
| 16. The demand for pet services — including insurance, training, grooming, breeding, pet rentals, and pet shows — at least doubles | 80 |
| 17. Home breeding of endangered animal species becomes a widespread hobby of environmentally conscious Americans | 70 |

example, highly likely to occur, likely to occur, 50/50 chance of occurring, and so forth) or quantitatively on a scale of zero (impossible to happen) to one hundred (certain to occur). Remember, a probability assessment assumes only that the development will occur at some point in the time horizon of interest (seventeen years ahead for Prime Pet Foods).

A more precise restatement of the developments in Table 5.1 appears in Table 5.2, along with a quantitative assessment of their likelihood of occurrence on a scale from zero to one hundred.

As you look over your list of key developments and their probabilities, you may see the outlines of a vision statement beginning to form. For example, even a cursory review of Table 5.2 suggests some implications for a new vision for Prime Pet Foods:

■   Much higher standards for pet food processing are likely, necessitating substantial investments in new plants and equipment if Prime continues its current product lines (Items 1, 14, and 15).

- The nature of the pet population is likely to change, requiring a substantial change in Prime's traditional product mix (Items 5, 6, 13, and 17).

- Nonfood pet markets are likely to expand at a much higher rate than the pet food products, creating new opportunities for well-established brand names like Prime (Items 3, 7, and 16).

- Much tougher competitive conditions are likely in the domestic pet food market (Items 2, 9, 11, and 12).

- New channels of distribution for pet foods are likely to open up, reducing the value of Prime's competitive advantage in supermarkets (Items 4 and 10).

To this point, you have been thinking about individual developments that could shape the future for your organization. Now you need to weave them together into holistic images or scenarios.

# BUILDING SCENARIOS

One day not long ago I was musing about the human tendency to think about the future in small disconnected fragments. Why is it that we are so willing to develop forecasts and to extrapolate trends but then so rarely take the time to put the pieces together and think about how they relate to each other? Is it any wonder, then, that leaders often seem to be missing the forest for the trees? It is the pattern, not the pieces, that matter, especially in developing a new vision for your organization; after all, the essence of the visioning process is finding a place for your organization in that pattern. This line of thinking inspired me to write a short poem.

"The Big Picture"

See the whole picture; Adjust the lens
to see the stars far and deep.

Let the wide angle admit
all of life's light and shadows.

See the whole picture; Focus the mind's eye
like a spotlight on the inner stage.
Only with eyes shut tight
can there be the brilliant insight.

See the whole picture; Scan the edges,
for meaning may not lie in the center.
As the sculpture is revealed in its form
and the sea defined by its shore.

See the whole picture; Study the dreams
of the great dreamers and sages.
Thus did Martin, through Gandhi's eyes,
see freedom in Montgomery's masses.

Now —
See the whole picture.

The best way to see the whole picture for our purposes is to combine the individual expectations into scenarios. A scenario is a story or verbal tapestry woven out of the individual expectations that is plausible and internally consistent. Three or four scenarios are usually quite sufficient to encompass a representative range of future outcomes.

The best way to start to write a scenario is by reviewing the high-impact developments in Table 5.2 to pick some themes or "drivers." The themes should be distinctly different to encompass a range of alternatives for the future external environment, some good and some bad. In the Prime Pet Foods example, we might identify the following themes:

1. A business-as-usual scenario in which historic trends continue into the next two decades much as they have in the past

2. A market-driven scenario in which pet ownership expands faster than historic rates, producing a burst of new

marketing entries and channels to accommodate the growth

3.  An austerity scenario in which economic conditions worsen, with increasingly negative effects on pet ownership

4.  A technology-driven scenario in which new product and process breakthroughs alter the nature of the pet food industry

5.  A consumerist-driven scenario in which consumerists and environmentalists gain political clout, forcing heavier control and regulation of the pet food industry

6.  An international market–driven scenario in which developments in the international food business result in dramatic changes in the way pet food is marketed and in Prime's parent company's organization and operations

After identifying possible themes, select three or four of them that represent an appropriate range of outcomes. Then, separate the full list of expectations into the chosen three or four themes. It doesn't much matter if all the expectations are included, but those chosen for each scenario must be consistent with each other and with the theme itself.

When you've sorted out the lists, you can begin to write the scenarios. There are two main ways to do so. The scenario can be a narrative starting from the present and chronologically unfolding to the desired future time. Or it can be a description of the desired future time — say, the year 2010 — with perhaps a few backward glances about how the world got that way over the preceding two decades.

Writing scenarios is a highly creative act. Your list of expectations relating to each theme is just the starting point. As you look at each item, think about what it is, how it might have come about, and what might follow from it to shape the external environment of your organization. You will probably find it useful to add other developments as you go along and to elaborate on the general conditions of the larger society. Weave together a credible tale so that when it is finished, a reasonable person would say that it makes sense — that is, that the world could indeed evolve as the scenario suggests.

Four to six paragraphs are usually quite sufficient to convey the nature of a particular scenario. Don't worry about writing a prophetic scenario; don't try to produce an accurate depiction of what will be, only of what could be. Like your anticipations themselves, a scenario cannot be judged right or wrong in advance since the events depicted haven't happened yet (and may never happen). A scenario can only be more or less useful for developing your vision, and for this purpose plausibility and credibility are the proper criteria.

Suppose we decided to develop three scenarios for use in the Prime Pet Foods example and chose themes 1, 2, and 4 of the six identified above. Here are the scenarios that might result, with the numbers and letters in parentheses showing where the developments were identified earlier in the chapter.

### Scenario 1. Business as Usual, 2010

As the year 2010 begins, it is apparent that muddling through has taken its toll on the U.S. economy. The frequent "small wars" of the past two decades in the Middle East and Central America, combined with the continued instability of Central Europe and China, have sapped U.S. resources and energy. The failure to invest sufficiently in infrastructure and education in the 1980s and 1990s has come home to roost in declining American competitiveness. When this decline became clear by the turn of the century, Americans tried to continue borrowing from foreigners to maintain their standard of living. But they found fewer and fewer lenders, which drove up interest rates (3a) and further taxed their economy. This drove up all costs, including food (3d) and energy (3c), and caused frequent recessionary cycles (3b).

Socially, the trends toward more retired people, smaller families, and more working wives continue. Politically, budgets are tight at every level of government, and tougher regulation has been extended to environmental controls on dust, noise, odors, and waste control (5a) and has led to new employer requirements in such areas as worker health and safety (5e).

Trends in pet ownership are consistent with the above. Economic pressure has cut pet ownership (3b) and led to smaller square footage in family homes, so the pet ownership that does exist has moved away from dogs (especially large dogs) (2f) toward cats, birds, and small mammals and reptiles (2g). Continued world famines only reinforce this trend because they have made the ownership of large pets by Americans appear to be insensitive, self-indulgent, and wasteful of food that should be used for human consumption (3e). In fact, government agencies seem to agree, since there are now luxury taxes on pets and pet foods, much higher licensing fees for pet owners (5b), and increased prohibition of pets in certain areas, for example, condos and parks (4a).

The high cost of living has caused many pet owners to seek cheaper feeding alternatives, so high-priced meat formulas have lost market share to protein analogs (6a), and supermarkets devote increased shelf space to lower-cost but higher-margin house brands instead of national brands (2a). At the same time, supermarkets have put more pressure on pet food companies to spend more on advertising and in-store promotion of pet foods (2c).

In the pet food industry, there is greater concentration, with a shakeout of marginal performers, and more national brands at the expense of local brands (2xx). The costs of new product introduction have increased considerably, including market research, testing, and advertising (2z), and so have labor costs, due to higher benefit costs resulting from increased worker entitlements (2q). These cost pressures, along with higher interest, energy, and food costs, have led to much higher levels of automation in pet food processing to increase productivity, product yields, and quality control (6d).

Prime Pet Foods might benefit from having access to

funds from the parent company at a time when interest rates are high (3a). With the pet food market stagnant or declining, however, the parent company sees much better investment opportunities in more robust overseas markets and has been treating Prime as a cash cow, reducing the portion of Prime's own cash flow that it can retain for investment (2m). At last, the parent company merges Prime with other U.S. food subsidiaries to achieve efficiencies and leverage its clout with supermarkets and the advertising media (2n).

### Scenario 2.  Market Driven, 2010

As the year 2010 begins, it is apparent that the United States has been able to manage its economic and political concerns over the past two decades somewhat better than expected. The large foreign debts incurred by the United States in the 1980s and early 1990s were reduced by an annual inflation rate exceeding 6 percent per year and a surprisingly robust American export effort that took advantage of the inability of the European Community to rationalize its members' national differences and interests and the Japanese stock market crash of 1995, after which Japan turned inward for almost a decade. With massive internal problems, non-Communist Central Europe and much of the Middle East avoided adventures outside their borders for the past two decades. Except for a few minor skirmishes in Central and South America, the United States has been able to avoid wars and to redirect much of its defense budget to domestic concerns, investing especially in education and infrastructure.

The robust U.S. economy, stimulated by the export boom and helped by energy and food prices that have increased less than inflation, has produced a substantial rise in the American standard of living. The effects have not all been beneficial, however. With drug problems, delinquency, and crime rates continuing to increase, many professionals and more affluent Americans — especially those able to take advantage of the increasingly sophisticated computers and telecommunications that facilitate working at home or in distant resort areas (4b)—have sought safety by moving from larger cities to smaller communities. The remaining urban areas, deprived of many of their brightest and more affluent taxpayers, are now mainly the homes of the aged poor, recently arrived immigrants, and low-wage service and production workers. Services are poor in these large cities, and crime rates are such that most cities impose strict curfews at night to protect their citizens.

In this environment, pet ownership has expanded considerably. In the larger cities, more dogs are used for protection and patrol purposes (4d). In rural areas, the telecommuters seek pets to relieve their loneliness and sense of isolation (4b), and many individuals seek pedigree pets that are treated as family members and displayed at local and regional shows (1a). Pet companionship has been found highly beneficial by the aged and the growing population of retired baby boomers (4c). There is also a substantial amount of home breeding of endangered animal species by affluent environmentally conscious Americans (7e).

The pet industry has prospered in this environment. Many new niches have opened up as pet owners seek more peoplelike foods for their pampered pets (1g) and more convenience in packaging and self-feeding (1e). The market for "treats" such as dog biscuits and cat snacks has been the fastest growing segment of the pet food industry (1d) for nearly a decade and now commands almost as much shelf space as more conventional foods. In fact, all pet products, not just foods, are in great demand. Affluent professionals who treat their pets like children buy huge quantities of pet clothes, toys, accessories, and grooming supplies (2h), and these items are widely sold in supermarkets (2d). Other services—like pet insurance, pet-sitting while owners travel (2j), training, grooming, breeding, pet rentals, and pet shows (7b)—are also in demand. In addition, education about pets is a significant market, with pet owners buying books, videotapes, and computer programs and enrolling in pet care and training classes (7d).

In response to this demand, some supermarkets, having expanded their store size, now include pet store boutiques (2e). A national chain of pet supermarkets has been franchised, offering discount prices on pet products, including foods (7c). Pet foods are also being distributed through new outlets, such as gasoline stations, hardware stores, and pet supply stores in shopping centers (2yy). Two major consumer firms, Procter & Gamble and Lever Brothers, have entered the pet food business (2y).

With this robust activity in the United States, Prime Pet Foods' parent company has decided to merge its pet food subsidiaries in other countries into Prime to form an international pet food powerhouse that shares brands and research capabilities (2l). This allows the parent company to adopt Prime's products and brand names for expansion into new overseas markets (2o) and also makes new foreign products available to Prime for sale in the United States.

### Scenario 3. Technology Driven, 2010

As the year 2010 begins, the economic and political circumstances are largely as described in the business-as-usual scenario. In other words, the United States is under considerable economic stress in an aggressively competitive and hostile world. As a result, overall real economic growth in the United States lags behind that of its major competitor nations. The big difference is that the social consolidation and political moderation of the 1990s gave way to a decade of social activism (reminiscent of the 1960s) starting at the turn of the century. Unsolved issues like minority rights, homelessness, and poverty are still matters of concern, but the major emphasis of activists centers on three fronts: the problems of the elderly, who now represent a major voting bloc; the problems of children, who are seen by many as disadvantaged, disenfranchised losers in an intergenerational struggle for resources; and environmental issues, which have come to the fore as a result of several ecodisasters in the United States. An activist "New Wave" president was elected in 2000, and shortly after that, systems of national planning and national health insurance were initiated.

All this political activism made an impact on the pet food industry, which has been the target of many class action suits to pursue consumerist and environmentalist agendas (5d). Tougher standards were established on all foods, including pet foods, to control quality, nutrition, and environmental impacts. Among the changes were tighter regulations on the use of animal by-products, advertising claims, labeling, and the use of chemical additives (5c).

The pet food industry responded with a wave of technological innovations. It developed nutritious new products, such as special diet foods (1h), added safe drugs to pet foods to control allergies, fleas, and other pet maladies (6c), and replaced the tin can with a variety of new packaging alternatives and food preservation methods (6b). Since animal by-products had become much more expensive as human meat consumption decreased (7a), the industry developed protein analog substitutes that were less expensive, more palatable, and environmentally benign (6a). With great progress in medicine and biotechnology, the industry's researchers were able to better understand and provide for nutritional balance (6e), make important breakthroughs in pet longevity (1b), and begin to genetically engineer pets to eliminate diseases and optimize desirable characteristics (6f).

Information technologies also made their contributions to the industry. Supermarkets were better able to track brand movement and allocate shelf space (2b), and fewer levels of management were needed due to factory automation and powerful communications devices (2v). In fact, technology became a major competitive weapon in the industry and was almost as important as marketing in determining company success. This, plus the fact that the pet food industry itself was not growing very fast, led to a shakeout in the industry, with only the largest and strongest — that is, those most able to invest in plant automation, research, and new product innovation — left to compete. Prime's parent company decided it could use its resources better elsewhere and sold the division (2k) to Johnson & Johnson, which had the needed research capability and was looking for a greater presence in supermarket chains for its health care lines.

# DRAWING IMPLICATIONS

With three or four scenarios of the future external environment of your organization, you are now in a position to draw some tentative conclusions for your vision statement. One way to do this is to review each scenario separately and ask yourself how you would position your organization to take the greatest advantage of that particular scenario. Another approach is to identify the strengths and weaknesses of your organization as currently configured to deal with each scenario. These approaches may suggest changes in direction to overcome your organization's weaknesses or build on its strengths.

For example, the president of Prime Pet Foods might review these scenarios and reason as follows:

### Scenario 1. Business as Usual

*1.* The high economic stress in this scenario would probably give a market advantage to low-priced pet food products. We have a good cost position now, but any further cost lowering would require large investments in automation by the parent company, and they're unlikely to want to do so if the overall market is not growing much and our market share continues to decline. Besides, our larger competitors have economy-of-scale advantages we can't hope to match. Therefore, we'd better avoid positioning ourselves as the low-priced pet food producer.

2.    The market in this scenario is moving heavily to smaller animals like cats. Perhaps we should start right now to emphasize the cat food market and then gradually introduce pet foods for other small animals as well. In fact, maybe we could even promote ownership of small animals, such as hamsters and rabbits, and position ourselves to be the principal food supplier.

3.    If things go as badly for the United States as this scenario suggests, our parent company may begin to lose interest in us and start treating us like a cash cow. Maybe we could prevent that by moving our cash flow, while we still control it, into product lines in faster growth areas or higher-margin products like pet accessories. We have good brand names and excellent supermarket contacts to build on.

4.    Our larger competitors would not like to promote the use of house brands by supermarket chains because they stand to lose the most from that. Perhaps this represents an opportunity for us to gain some volume and lower our costs by aggressively promoting ourselves to that market and starting a house brands line.

### Scenario 2. Market Driven

1.    In a robust market as described in this scenario, it is likely that large new competitors, perhaps even from overseas, will be attracted to enter the pet food market. We don't want to get into a spending war with these giants, so perhaps we should increasingly position ourselves for niches that big companies wouldn't find attractive.

2.    This world envisions large telecommuter populations and other affluent people treating their dogs as people. This creates many niche markets in upscale pet foods—for example, gourmet pet foods, special dietary foods, foods geared to certain life stages ("puppies," "senior citizens"), or treats and

snacks (chips, cookies, candies)—where the margins would be higher and we might be able to dominate some segments. We have a strong market research department and a good research capability for this, and besides, we may be able to take advantage of products and brands in some of the other divisions of our parent company.

**3.**    If the market for pet foods expands as suggested, maybe we should take the initiative in proposing to establish pet boutiques for supermarkets or pet food sections in pet stores. By creating such facilities, we'll be in a position to ensure that our products get preferential exposure.

**4.**    The pet food business will always be highly competitive and subject to the low margins of supermarket chains. Maybe we should establish a division in the pet services business and try to find product niches in grooming, breeding, insurance, pet show products, books, and so forth.

### Scenario 3.  Technology Driven

*1.*    Prime is not now as innovative or risk-taking a company as some competitors. In this scenario, we would have to beef up our new product development and introduction capability, perhaps seeking closer ties with the research and development staffs of our parent company. We'd also have to change the culture of the organization to be more risk oriented, which might require substantial changes in staffing and organization.

**2.**    The environmental activism suggests many opportunities for Prime. Maybe we should establish a new label (Prime Green?) for a line of pet foods in environmentally responsible packaging (as opposed to tin cans) that features organic pet foods free of hormones and pesticides, protein analogs in place of meat by-products, and so forth.

**3.**    The concern with health and nutrition suggests a line of health-oriented foods, perhaps under a new brand (Dr.

Prime?), that includes dietetic foods, vitamins, drugs for minor ailments, and the like. If so, maybe we should consider either a joint venture with a leading pharmaceutical company on these products or perhaps just a research and licensing agreement.

As these examples show, there are visionary implications that apply to only one scenario and others that work in more than one. Ultimately, the best vision is the one that works across all the scenarios — or at least doesn't harm the organization's prospects no matter what happens.

As T. S. Eliot wrote in his poem "Burnt Norton," "Time past and time future / What might have been and what has been / Point to one end, which is always present." We have spent the last three chapters looking at time past and time future to bring them into time present. It remains now to put all the pieces together and come up with a new vision for your organization.

# CHAPTER 6

# Finding Your Way:
## The Vision Choice

My eyes already touch the sunny hill,
going far ahead of the road I have begun.
So we are grasped by what we cannot grasp;
it has its inner light, even from a distance—
and changes us, even if we do not reach it,
into something else, which, hardly sensing it,
    we already are;
a gesture waves us on, answering our own
    wave.
—Rainer Maria Rilke

Suppose you were faced with this challenge. Take a tiny, private, century-old Jesuit college with around one thousand students, buildings in disrepair, heavily in debt, and located in a city plagued by sick industries and rampant unemployment. Within a decade, convert it into a thriving university with eight thousand students, sparkling new buildings, a substantial budget surplus, eight new master's degree programs, and a reputation as an academic leader in its region. An impossible leadership task, you say? Perhaps, but that's precisely what Father David M. Clarke did when he became president of Regis University in Denver, Colorado.

How did he do it? His secret was visionary leadership of a high order. He looked around and saw what everyone else did: a declining number of eighteen-year-olds, the traditional population from which college students are recruited; vigorous competition from state universities, whose prestige, proliferation of course offerings, and subsidized degree programs made life miserable for a private college dependent on tuition income; rapidly increasing costs for qualified faculty, campus security, libraries, building maintenance, and other requirements of campus life; and not much hope of attracting substantial additional support from the small base of loyal, but already overtaxed, alumni. Business as usual, Father Clarke knew, was the path to certain financial ruin, a fate suffered by many other small colleges. Yet he also knew that most college presidents are convinced that changing a university is only slightly easier than moving a cemetery.

This much everyone saw, but Father Clarke saw something else as well. Education is a service business, he reasoned. If Regis University could not get enough traditional high school graduates to pay tuition to study there, perhaps there were other markets where Regis could carve out a niche. Father Clarke saw that the business recession in the Denver area was creating a need for many adults to learn new careers. He saw that local businesses needed to upgrade the skills of their workers in management, technology, communications, and languages in order to compete internationally. He saw that professional health care workers, teachers, accountants, and others also needed continuing education.

Ultimately, he put the pieces together in a creative way. He formulated a new vision for Regis University dedicated to serving the adult education market. The emphasis was to be on customer service, with courses, professors, and materials brought to adult students in their places of business and at other convenient locations on schedules tailored to their needs. Agreements were formed with local employers for Regis to take over in-house educational needs. Cost controls, salesmanship, quality control, and other standard business techniques were employed. Moreover, according to the *Wall Street Journal*, "Father Clarke insists that Regis's businesslike approach hasn't watered down academic standards. He notes that all of Regis's students, even those enrolled at IBM and Coors, must take the same philosophy and religion classes as its regular undergraduates" (Charlier, 1991, p. A5).

The result was not simply a dramatic turnaround or even

a new application for old professorial skills; it was a whole new direction for the institution. In fact, although it is 114-years-old, Regis University today is a new institution, vigorously growing to fill the niche created by its president's vision.

There would have been no vision had Father Clarke not thought deeply about his organization's current business, its strengths and weaknesses, its current direction, its culture, and its stakeholders. And there would have been no vision had he not been able to develop a good grasp of the changes occurring in Regis's external environments. But most of all, no vision existed until Father Clarke assembled all these observations and reflections and distilled them into a creative new direction for his university. Putting it all together is what this chapter is about.

# THE LEADER AS GREAT SYNTHESIZER

People who study and write about leadership often disagree on what makes for effective leadership. However, they all agree that leaders, at a minimum, are intelligent beings; some would say highly intelligent. In his remarkable Pulitzer Prize-winning book *Gödel, Escher, Bach*, Douglas Hofstadter (1980, p. 26) defines the essential abilities for intelligence as follows:

to respond to situations very flexibly;

to take advantage of fortuitous circumstances;

to make sense out of ambiguous or contradictory messages;

to recognize the importance of different elements of a situation;

to find similarities between situations despite differences which may separate them;

to draw distinctions between situations despite similarities which may link them;

to synthesize new concepts by taking old concepts and putting them together in new ways;

to come up with ideas which are novel.

These are the very abilities needed to synthesize a vision. A great vision, of course, may demand exceptional creativity, intuition, judgment, or wisdom, but the basic abilities to formulate a vision clearly are well within the range of any intelligent person.

Synthesizing a vision often means developing a new pattern of relationships among old elements, much as Father Clarke did for Regis University. Each person does that differently, of course, but I have found the following steps helpful:

1. Review the materials you have assembled in response to the questions in the earlier chapters with an open mind. That is, do not rush to judgment or try to figure out immediately what it all adds up to. Just let it cook in your mind for awhile. Stay flexible, but write down any thoughts or ideas that might flash by at unpredictable moments — while driving to work or exercising or perhaps while relaxing late at night.

2. Build a mental map of the whole domain of possible visions. Usually there are several key dimensions that define the map — products and markets, for example, or in the case of Regis University, the nature of the student body and the nature of the curriculum being taught. Keep focusing on the long term and the big picture.

3. Generate a series of alternative visions, allowing yourself to try strange and exotic combinations. The more alternatives the better, and at this stage, don't be judgmental about them. Sometimes a totally impractical thought may spark another more acceptable one, or you may think of a way to make practical what seems at first to be a wild idea.

4. When you have a reasonable set of alternative visions, order the visions in terms of which seem most promising. Then, starting at the top of the list, test the vision alternatives against the desired properties of a good vision, the measures of success generated earlier, and consistency with your organization's culture, values, strengths, and stakeholders and with the scenarios of your organization's future external environment. Don't reject an idea simply because it fails one or a few tests. Often a slight modification of a vision or perhaps a merging of two or three visions will deal with any shortcomings you identify.

5. State the vision as clearly as you can and discuss it with several trusted colleagues. Listen carefully to their responses, noting particularly any unintended interpretations or implications of your vision, and modify your vision accordingly.

There is a limit to what can be done with a strictly rational approach, of course, and you should be open to those mysterious flashes of insight that often come when people immerse themselves in interesting and important issues. You should also be a good listener, for no two minds are exactly alike, even those of people who have been working together for years. Respected colleagues or friends may illuminate aspects of your vision that escaped your attention because you are so close to the matter yourself.

This chapter shows how to follow the above steps to generate a new vision, using the Prime Pet Foods example. As before, the book's Appendix shows how the same steps would be followed in the case of a public agency.

## MAPPING THE DOMAIN

Some years ago, I was invited to give a series of lectures in Australia. Several months before the trip, the sponsor of the lecture series called to make the final arrangements. He pointed out that although the lectures would be tightly scheduled in several different cities, there would be a free three-and-a-half-day weekend in the middle of the series. He asked whether there was anything in Australia I would particularly like to see or do during that time. Impulsively, I responded that I'd love to try some snorkling on the famous Great Barrier Reef. Without further comment, he cordially agreed to make the necessary arrangements. It was not until much later, long after the arrangements had been finalized, that I chanced to look at a map and discovered that to reach the Great Barrier Reef, I'd have to fly more than 1,200 miles each way from the site of my last address to get there. It actually took three flights in each direction, and the total time allotted for the trip was only three-and-a-half days!

Of course, I would not have signed up for such a hectic schedule had I simply taken a few minutes to look at a map before determining my destination. Just so, picking an organizational direction is much facilitated with a map. You're far more likely to end up at the right place and in good condition if you can draw a map of possible destinations ahead of time.

There are many ways to do so. One is to position your organization on a graph defining the major differentiating characteristics in your industry, as illustrated in Figure 6.1 for the automobile industry. In this sort of diagram, one is searching for unoccupied niches that may represent new market opportunities or unexplored destinations.

A second approach is to prepare a traditional growth vector analysis (Rowe, Mason, Dickel, and Snyder, 1989, p. 113) similar to the one shown in Figure 6.2 for the hospital industry.

A third way to map the domain is to analyze the distinctive competencies of the organization and then seek combinations that employ the largest number of such skills. For example, suppose an apparel manufacturer listed the skills at which she really excelled as follows:

**Figure 6.1. Organizational Positioning.**

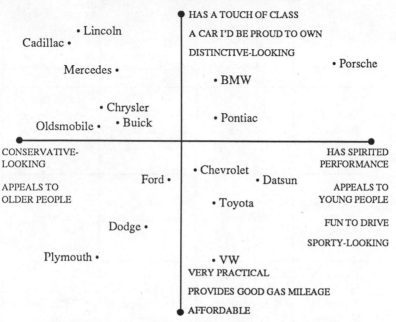

■ Designing clothes for small girls

■ Making play costumes

■ Cutting intricate patterns

■ Combining unconventional materials and colors

■ Marketing to upscale families

■ Clever packaging

Combining all or some of these skills would suggest new product/market directions that are not only feasible and attractive but will insulate the manufacturer from competition, since no other manufacturer is likely to excel at precisely the same set of skills.

### Figure 6.2. Growth Vector Analysis.

*Markets*

|  | Traditional Markets | Expanded Markets | New Markets |
|---|---|---|---|
| Current Products/ Services | Operating Rooms | Mobile Cancer Screening | Miniclinics in Large Firms |
| Expanded Products/ Services | Home Birthing Centers | Drug Rehabilitation Centers | Wellness Centers |
| New Products/ Services | Operations Recovery Hotel | Home Diagnostic Systems | Veterinary Centers |

*Products/Services*

A fourth approach derives from the notion that new directions are likely to arise either from advances in technology that affect products, services, or operating processes or from changes in the demand structure. These dimensions can be arranged in a two-by-two matrix as shown in Figure 6.3. Then, potential new directions can be entered into the boxes.

Finally, a sort of brute force method can be used in which major markets are listed across the top of a sheet of paper and products or services are listed down the side. Table 6.1 illustrates this method as it might be applied in the case of the pet food industry.

All of these methods enable you to develop a framework or mental model that lays out the big picture—that is, the space of possible visions. Now you are ready to begin to identify promising alternatives.

**Figure 6.3. Technology/Demand Matrix.**

*Demand Pull*

|  | From New Needs and Wants | From Environmental Changes |
|---|---|---|
| New Products or Services |  |  |
| New Operating Processes |  |  |

*Technology Push*

# GENERATING ALTERNATIVE VISIONS

No organization, no matter how large or versatile, can be all things to all people. If a hospital tries to serve all the medical needs of its community, it will soon spread itself too thin and fail to serve well those who need it the most. No matter how large a corporation is – even one as huge as IBM or AT&T – it must choose its product lines and target markets carefully or competitors will chip away at it by serving specific markets better. Even the United States government, with all the resources it commands, cannot do everything its citizens demand of it; indeed, there are many who delight in pointing out its many inadequacies.

Since the same limitations are certainly true for your own organization, your task now is to answer the following question: "Of all the possible directions we could take over the next five to seven years, which ones offer the greatest promise of

Table 6.1. Product/Market Matrix for the Pet Food Industry.

| | Cat owners | Dog owners | Other pet owners | Nonpet animal owners | Kennels and other institutions | Vets |
|---|---|---|---|---|---|---|
| 1. Moist foods | • | • | • | | • | • |
| 2. Semimoist foods | • | • | • | | • | • |
| 3. Dry foods | • | • | • | • | • | |
| 4. Treats | • | • | • | | • | • |
| 5. Litter | • | | | | • | • |
| 6. Decorative accessories | • | • | • | | • | • |
| 7. Hygienic accessories | • | • | • | | • | • |
| 8. Health items | • | • | • | • | • | • |
| 9. Fresh foods | • | • | • | | | |
| 10. Frozen foods | • | • | | | | |
| 11. Medicated foods | • | • | • | • | • | • |
| 12. Liquid foods | • | • | • | | • | |
| 13. Age-specific foods | • | • | • | • | • | • |
| 14. Gifts/toys | • | • | • | | • | • |
| 15. Insurance | • | • | • | • | • | • |
| 16. Grooming items | • | • | • | • | • | • |
| 17. Boarding services | • | • | • | • | • | |
| 18. Shelter/cages | • | • | • | • | • | • |
| 19. Scrap enhancers | • | • | • | • | | |
| 20. Pet sales | • | • | • | | • | |
| 21. Education/classes/books | • | • | • | • | • | • |
| 22. Animal training | • | • | | | • | |
| 23. Pet shows | • | • | • | • | | |
| 24. Bulk foods | | | | • | • | |
| 25. Rental pets | • | • | • | | | |
| 26. Pet medicines | • | • | • | • | • | • |
| 27. Medical tests and equipment | | | | • | • | • |
| 28. Photos/videos/albums | • | • | | | | |

dramatically improving our position and achieving the greatest success for us and for our key stakeholders?" Drawing on all your accumulated experience and wisdom, using the information generated in response to the questions of the earlier chapters, and developing a framework from one of the methods presented in the prior section, you must now prepare a list of the most attractive possible visions for your organization.

This is the magic moment when it all comes together — information, mental model, experience, values, judgment, and intuition — all interacting in a creative mental stew. It is the point at which left-brain thinking (linear, analytical, data oriented) and right-brain thinking (holistic, intuitive, image oriented) unite as your mind attempts to synthesize a possible vision statement for your organization. This is a highly creative process, and you may wish to prepare for it by reading about techniques that writers, artists, and other creative people use to stimulate their thoughts when faced by a challenging problem (see, for example, Rico, 1983; Shekerjian, 1990; Gardner, 1982).

My suggestion is that you start by brainstorming a list of possible candidates — no holding back, no premature criticism, no concern yet about feasibility or acceptability — simply a listing of dreams. If it helps you through this process, try to list alternative ways to end the following sentence: "My organization intends to make enormous progress over the next ——— years by ———." Here are some examples how a leader at Prime Pet foods might complete that sentence:

Prime Pet Foods intends to make enormous progress over the next seven years by...

1.  Becoming the national leader in gourmet foods, upscale accessories, and health products for pedigree and show pets

2.  Specializing in foods for cats, small dogs, and other small mammals

3. Extending our well-established brands into specialty pet food niches such as treats, cookies, scrap enhancers, age-specific foods, medicated foods, and vitamins

4. Forming a joint venture with a leading pharmaceutical company to specialize in dietary pet foods, health items, pet medicines, and medical testing

5. Building a chain of pet service boutiques, some free-standing, some in hypermarkets or department stores, to offer pet foods, gifts, and accessories along with a range of grooming, insurance, education, training, and photographic services

6. Becoming known as the socially responsible pet food company by excelling in health, dietary, and environmental quality in all pet food products

7. Harnessing the research capacity of our parent company to become the innovation leader in our industry, with the goal of no more than 40 percent of our revenues in seven years coming from existing product lines

8. Striving to be the low-cost leader in the pet food industry, capturing the major part of the bulk food and house brand markets

Obviously, many more viable directions could be developed for Prime Pet Foods, but let's proceed to the next step.

## CHOOSING THE RIGHT VISION

Sometimes the best vision seems intuitively obvious, but even so, it is worth checking it, as well as the other major contenders, against the criteria developed in the earlier chapters. The first set of criteria (see Chapter Two) concerned the properties of a good vision, which are summarized below:

■   To what extent is it *future oriented?*

■   To what extent is it *utopian* — that is, is it likely to lead to a clearly better future for the organization?

■   To what extent is it *appropriate* for the organization — that is, does it fit in with the organization's history, culture, and values?

■   To what extent does it set standards of excellence and *reflect high ideals?*

■   To what extent does it *clarify purpose* and direction?

■   To what extent is it likely to *inspire enthusiasm* and encourage commitment?

■   To what extent does it *reflect the uniqueness* of the organization, its distinctive competence and what it stands for?

■   Is it *ambitious* enough?

In Table 6.2, the eight alternative visions for Prime Pet Foods identified in the last section are evaluated against these criteria, using a scale of 1 to 5, where 5 represents the highest degree of compliance possible. However, in Table 6.2, all the criteria were weighted equally in importance. Usually, some criteria are more important than the others, and so we prepare a second evaluation, illustrated in Table 6.3, in which relative weights on a scale of 1 to 10 are assigned to each criterion, where 10 is the most important. The entries in Table 6.3 show the value obtained by multiplying the criterion importance weighting times the compliance ratings shown in Table 6.2. When the totals are summed at the bottom of each column, they show the relative attractiveness of each alternative. Clearly, alternative 7 has the highest total and fits these weighted criteria best.

The next step is to compare each of the alternatives with the measures of success developed in Chapter Four. For

Table 6.2. How Good Are the Vision Statements?

| | Alternatives | | | | | | | |
|---|---|---|---|---|---|---|---|---|
| Criteria | 1 | 2 | 3 | 4 | 5 | 6 | 7 | 8 |
| Future oriented? | 5 | 5 | 5 | 5 | 4 | 5 | 5 | 3 |
| Utopian? | 4 | 3 | 4 | 4 | 4 | 4 | 5 | 3 |
| Appropriate? | 2 | 4 | 4 | 2 | 2 | 4 | 5 | 3 |
| Reflects high ideals? | 3 | 3 | 4 | 4 | 3 | 5 | 5 | 4 |
| Clarifies purpose? | 5 | 5 | 4 | 4 | 4 | 4 | 5 | 4 |
| Inspires enthusiasm? | 4 | 3 | 4 | 4 | 3 | 4 | 5 | 4 |
| Reflects uniqueness? | 3 | 4 | 4 | 3 | 3 | 4 | 5 | 2 |
| Ambitious? | 3 | 3 | 4 | 5 | 5 | 4 | 5 | 5 |

Prime Pet Foods, the measures of success were: sales growth, profits growth, innovation, product diversity, customer satisfaction, and high product quality and value. These comparisons are made in Table 6.4 using the same 1 to 5 scale. Table 6.5 assumes that all the measures of success are not equally important to Prime. Thus, as before, this table weights each measure of success on a scale of 1 to 10, multiplies that rating by the scores in Table 6.4, and totals them to get a new evaluation. Here again, alternative 7 received the highest total score, although alternative 4 is close behind.

Table 6.3. Vision Statements with Weighted Criteria.

| | Relative | Alternatives | | | | | | | |
|---|---|---|---|---|---|---|---|---|---|
| Criteria | Weight | 1 | 2 | 3 | 4 | 5 | 6 | 7 | 8 |
| Future oriented? | (9) | 45 | 45 | 45 | 45 | 36 | 45 | 45 | 27 |
| Utopian? | (7) | 28 | 21 | 28 | 28 | 28 | 28 | 35 | 21 |
| Appropriate? | (7) | 14 | 28 | 28 | 14 | 14 | 28 | 35 | 21 |
| Reflects high ideals? | (9) | 27 | 27 | 36 | 36 | 27 | 45 | 45 | 36 |
| Clarifies purpose? | (10) | 50 | 50 | 40 | 40 | 40 | 40 | 50 | 40 |
| Inspires enthusiasm? | (8) | 32 | 24 | 32 | 32 | 24 | 32 | 40 | 32 |
| Reflects uniqueness? | (6) | 18 | 24 | 24 | 18 | 18 | 24 | 30 | 12 |
| Ambitious? | (8) | 24 | 24 | 32 | 40 | 40 | 32 | 40 | 40 |
| Totals | | 238 | 243 | 265 | 253 | 227 | 274 | 320 | 229 |

Table 6.4. Comparing Alternatives with Measures of Success.

| Measures of Success | Alternatives | | | | | | | |
|---|---|---|---|---|---|---|---|---|
| | 1 | 2 | 3 | 4 | 5 | 6 | 7 | 8 |
| Sales growth | 3 | 4 | 4 | 4 | 5 | 4 | 5 | 5 |
| Profits growth | 4 | 3 | 4 | 5 | 3 | 3 | 5 | 3 |
| Innovation | 4 | 2 | 4 | 5 | 5 | 4 | 5 | 2 |
| Product diversity | 4 | 4 | 5 | 5 | 5 | 4 | 5 | 2 |
| Customer satisfaction | 5 | 3 | 5 | 5 | 4 | 5 | 5 | 5 |
| High product quality and value | 5 | 3 | 4 | 5 | 4 | 5 | 5 | 5 |

Finally, it is necessary to evaluate the extent to which each alternative is consistent with other organizational factors established in earlier chapters, especially the following:

The organization's culture and values

The organization's strengths

The needs and expectations of major stakeholders

Supermarkets

Pet owners

The parent company

Table 6.5. Weighted Comparisons with Measures of Success.

| Measures of Success | Relative Weight | Alternatives | | | | | | | |
|---|---|---|---|---|---|---|---|---|---|
| | | 1 | 2 | 3 | 4 | 5 | 6 | 7 | 8 |
| Sales growth | (7) | 21 | 28 | 28 | 28 | 35 | 28 | 35 | 35 |
| Profits growth | (9) | 36 | 27 | 36 | 45 | 27 | 27 | 45 | 27 |
| Innovation | (8) | 32 | 16 | 32 | 40 | 40 | 32 | 40 | 16 |
| Product diversity | (8) | 32 | 32 | 40 | 40 | 40 | 32 | 40 | 16 |
| Customer satisfaction | (10) | 50 | 30 | 50 | 50 | 40 | 50 | 50 | 50 |
| High product quality and value | (8) | 40 | 24 | 32 | 40 | 32 | 40 | 40 | 40 |
| Totals | | 211 | 157 | 218 | 243 | 214 | 209 | 250 | 184 |

Workers

Managers

Scenarios of future environments

Business as usual

Market driven

Technology driven

This evaluation is performed in Table 6.6, which uses the same 1 to 5 scale, and in Table 6.7, in which the relative importance of the various components of organizational synergy to Prime Pet Foods is weighted on a scale of 1 to 10, as before. Here again, alternative 7 stands out.

For a final reckoning using this approach, Table 6.8 summarizes the totals from Tables 6.3, 6.5, and 6.7. As expected, alternative 7 is the clear winner, but now we need to take a closer look at the runners-up, alternatives 6, 3, and 4.

Table 6.6. Comparing Alternatives on Organizational Synergy.

| | Alternatives | | | | | | | |
|---|---|---|---|---|---|---|---|---|
| *Consistency with* | 1 | 2 | 3 | 4 | 5 | 6 | 7 | 8 |
| Organization's culture and values | 3 | 4 | 3 | 2 | 2 | 4 | 3 | 5 |
| Organization's strengths | 2 | 3 | 3 | 3 | 2 | 3 | 5 | 4 |
| Stakeholder needs | | | | | | | | |
|   Supermarkets | 3 | 4 | 3 | 2 | 1 | 4 | 5 | 5 |
|   Pet owners | 3 | 3 | 3 | 3 | 4 | 4 | 5 | 5 |
|   Parent company | 3 | 3 | 4 | 3 | 4 | 4 | 5 | 2 |
|   Workers | 4 | 3 | 3 | 3 | 2 | 4 | 4 | 2 |
|   Managers | 5 | 3 | 4 | 4 | 4 | 4 | 5 | 2 |
| Scenarios of the future | | | | | | | | |
|   Business as usual | 2 | 5 | 3 | 2 | 2 | 3 | 3 | 5 |
|   Market driven | 4 | 2 | 4 | 4 | 4 | 4 | 5 | 3 |
|   Technology driven | 3 | 3 | 5 | 5 | 3 | 5 | 5 | 2 |

Table 6.7. Weighted Comparisons on Organizational Synergy.

| Consistency with | Relative Weight | Alternatives | | | | | | | |
|---|---|---|---|---|---|---|---|---|---|
| | | 1 | 2 | 3 | 4 | 5 | 6 | 7 | 8 |
| Organization's culture and values | (10) | 30 | 40 | 30 | 20 | 20 | 40 | 30 | 50 |
| Organization's strengths | (8) | 16 | 24 | 24 | 24 | 16 | 24 | 40 | 32 |
| Stakeholder needs | | | | | | | | | |
| Supermarkets | (9) | 27 | 36 | 27 | 18 | 9 | 36 | 45 | 45 |
| Pet owners | (10) | 30 | 30 | 30 | 30 | 40 | 40 | 50 | 50 |
| Parent company | (10) | 30 | 30 | 40 | 30 | 40 | 40 | 50 | 20 |
| Workers | (8) | 32 | 24 | 24 | 24 | 16 | 32 | 32 | 16 |
| Managers | (8) | 40 | 24 | 32 | 32 | 32 | 32 | 40 | 16 |
| Scenarios of the future | | | | | | | | | |
| Business as usual | (8) | 16 | 40 | 24 | 16 | 16 | 24 | 24 | 40 |
| Market driven | (8) | 32 | 16 | 32 | 32 | 32 | 32 | 40 | 24 |
| Technology driven | (7) | 21 | 21 | 35 | 35 | 21 | 35 | 35 | 14 |
| Totals | | 274 | 285 | 298 | 261 | 242 | 335 | 386 | 307 |

# PACKAGING THE VISION

Up to this point, we have been following a logical—some might even say, overly analytical—approach to developing a vision. One way or another—quantitatively (as shown above), qualitatively, or strictly on the basis of judgment and intuition—you should have reached a general sense of direction. In

Table 6.8. Summing the Evaluations of Alternatives.

| Totals from | Alternatives | | | | | | | |
|---|---|---|---|---|---|---|---|---|
| | 1 | 2 | 3 | 4 | 5 | 6 | 7 | 8 |
| Table 6.3 | 238 | 243 | 265 | 253 | 227 | 274 | 320 | 229 |
| Table 6.5 | 211 | 157 | 218 | 243 | 214 | 209 | 250 | 184 |
| Table 6.7 | 274 | 285 | 298 | 261 | 242 | 335 | 386 | 307 |
| Totals | 723 | 685 | 781 | 757 | 683 | 818 | 956 | 720 |

the case of Prime Pet Foods, it is alternative 7, which was defined earlier as "harnessing the research capacity of our parent company to become the innovation leader in our industry, with the goal of no more than 40 percent of our revenues in seven years coming from existing product lines."

But rarely is the choice so definitive. In the Prime example, three other alternatives received high ratings: 6 ("becoming known as the socially responsible pet food company by excelling in health, dietary, and environmental quality in all pet food products"); 3 ("extending our well-established brands into specialty pet food niches such as treats, cookies, scrap enhancers, age-specific foods, medicated foods, and vitamins"); and 4 ("forming a joint venture with a leading pharmaceutical company to specialize in dietary pet foods, health items, pet medicines, and medical testing"). A stronger vision statement would be one that unites several of these themes, so let's try some different packages:

1.  Prime Pet Foods aspires to be the research leader in developing and distributing pet food and health care products that set high standards for value, quality, variety, and social responsibility. By the year 2000, at least 60 percent of its revenues should be from innovative products not now available. (Captures the essence of the vision, though perhaps a bit wordy.)

2.  Prime Pet Foods seeks excellence through innovation in a wide range of specialty food and health care products for family pets. (Simpler statement, but a bit flat.)

3.  Prime Pet Foods will provide outstanding quality and value to pet owners in a diverse, innovative line of pet food and health care products. (Stresses value to customers, but not as well focused on innovation as statement 1.)

4.  Prime Pet Foods seeks to enhance the value of pet ownership through a deep commitment to the individual health, happiness, and dietary needs of family pets, for

which it will provide a steady stream of innovative new food and health care products. (An improved variation of statement 3.)

5.  Prime Pet Foods seeks to be the research leader in developing and distributing pet food and health care products that enhance the value of pet ownership and set high standards for value, quality, variety, and social responsibility. (Combines statements 1 and 4.)

6.  Prime Pet Foods aspires to be the most innovative and socially responsible firm in its industry, dedicated to only one thing—the care and nourishment of the healthiest pets in the world. By the year 2000, at least 60 percent of its revenues will be from a variety of innovative, high-quality pet food and health care products not currently available. (Combines statements 1 and 5.)

Obviously, other variations are possible, but these examples are sufficient to demonstrate that there are many ways to package a vision. The choice of the final vision statement depends on what the leader feels will be most effective in his or her organization's culture—that is, the statement that will best capture the attention of the people in the organization by being meaningful, compelling, and appealing on both a rational and an emotional level. In the case of Prime Pet Foods, statement 5 or 6 may do this best. They both feature the theme of innovation in the context of a meaningful social purpose while also directing attention to a new agenda for the company—that is, through research to develop quality food and health care products for pets that are highly valued, niche-oriented (diverse), socially responsible, and enhance the value of pet ownership.

Some vision statements go one step further and attempt to encapsulate the vision in a short metaphor, slogan, or memorable statement that conveys its essence and captures attention. For example, when a new leader was chosen for John Wanamaker, a famous but failing department store in downtown Philadelphia, his vision for the future was of the store as theater (Trachtenberg, 1991). With the store's grand marble columns, a giant pipe organ that was played twice a day by a full-time organist, light shows, fountains, and restaurants, he saw John Wanamaker as a dramatic place that would use spectacle to attract people for a happy experience and then sell them with broad merchandise selection and service.

Is there a similar metaphor that captures the theme of Prime's vision statement? Perhaps it is nature itself, or Mother Earth, carefully protecting her creatures, bountiful and nurturing, always changing and evolving. This could be a symbol encapsulating the spirit of the new vision.

Was it worth all this trouble? Often, after a decision is made on a new vision, it appears painfully obvious in retrospect, and you may be forgiven for wondering why so much work had to be done just to get to this point. But if you look back at the path just taken, you will see that nearly as important as the final vision are all the alternatives eliminated by the process. For example, Prime Pet Food has decided not to

Continue in its current direction

Emphasize bulk and low-priced products

Emphasize upscale and gourmet pet food items

Focus on pet services

Produce foods for farm animals

Sell decorative items, pet toys, photographs, and the like

Open pet boutiques

All of these alternatives had a certain amount of appeal when first proposed and could have been chosen as the new direction, but all were found wanting compared to the final choice. Of course, they may not be entirely excluded. For example, Prime may still wish to offer gourmet products but only if it fits the other parts of the vision statement — high-quality, innovative, healthy, and so on. Moreover, these other alternatives may not be rejected forever. The leader needs to continually monitor market conditions and other circumstances and may decide at some later time to revisit these options (see Chapter Eight for further discussion on revisioning).

For now, if you have been following along, you have arrived at last at a new vision. A long process of data gathering, analysis, and judgment has led to your conclusion on a new sense of direction for your organization. You would do well at this point to pause and reflect on the new vision to make sure it is one that can arouse commitment and enthusiasm—first and foremost your own. Before others can be expected to buy into a new direction, you must be absolutely convinced in your own mind that it is right for the times, right for the environment, and right for your organization and everyone associated with it. Max DePree, himself an outstanding leader at the Herman Miller Company, likens the required level of the leader's personal commitment to that of Sir Christopher Wren, about whom he tells this story: "The noted English architect Sir Christopher Wren once built a structure in London. His employers claimed that a certain span Wren planned was too wide, that he would need another row of columns for support. Sir Christopher, after some discussion, acquiesced. He added the row of columns, but he left a space between the unnecessary columns and the beams above. The worthies of London could not see this space from the ground. To this day, the beam has not sagged. The columns still stand firm, supporting nothing but Wren's conviction" (1989, p. 135).

With a commitment as strong as that, you can't help but radiate optimism and enthusiasm for your new direction. But as Thomas Carlyle once said, "The end of man is an action, not a thought, though it were the noblest." It still remains for you to implement your vision, to convert it into reality, to literally make it happen. So now, as we leave the Prime Pet Foods example, we move on to the subjects of implementation and re-vision in Part Three.

# PART THREE

# Implementing the Vision

*The three chapters in
Part Three explore
how to turn a vision
into action and how
to decide when to
revise a vision.
Part Three concludes
with some thoughts
on the evolving role of
vision in leadership
and in organizations
of the future.*

# CHAPTER 7

# Making It Happen:
## Translating Vision into Reality

When it comes to the future,
there are three kinds of people:
    those who let it happen,
    those who make it happen,
and those who wonder what happened.
—JOHN M. RICHARDSON, JR.

Let anyone who still doubts the power of vision reflect for a moment on the modern miracle accomplished by German Chancellor Helmut Kohl in achieving the decades-old vision of unifying East and West Germany. The *Wall Street Journal* described the product of his leadership over a single momentous year as follows: "He unified Germany in such a way that he avoided arousing alarm abroad or nationalism at home. He kept unified Germany in the Western alliance, but he also forged closer relations with Moscow than at any time since the beginning of World War II. He made friends of Mr. Gorbachev, a man he once likened to Nazi propagandist Josef Goebbels, and he deployed his close relationship with George Bush to neutralize British and French misgivings about unification. Amid all this, he continued to press for European integration." (Kempe, 1990, p. A1).

Former French Foreign Minister Jean Francois Poncet marvels at Kohl's decisiveness in welding together two totally dissimilar socioeconomic systems so quickly, pointing out that "he has produced the image of a strong, powerful and rich Germany that is nevertheless democratic, pro-European and undangerous" (Kempe, 1990, p. A1).

The vision of a unified Germany had a powerful attraction for all Germans, of course, and some might think that Kohl simply seized the opportunity presented by a disintegrating Soviet Union to make it happen. Such a thought, however, grossly underestimates what it took to implement the vision. Kohl had to make the vision acceptable to all stakeholders, inside and outside of the two Germanys. He had to make a series of fateful decisions that radically altered the social, economic, and political landscape in West Germany — the free convertibility of the East German ostmark to marks, for example, or the grant of $20 billion in credits and subsidies to the Soviet Union to help ensure its endorsement. And he had to make important personnel changes in his own party and government and persuade or co-opt politicians and skeptics on both sides of the former Iron Curtain.

The vision — that beckoning target of German reunification — had been in existence for more than four decades. Kohl made the vision his own and then seized the moment to make it happen. In the process, he employed all the other roles of leadership discussed in Chapter One — spokesperson, change agent, and coach — to finally convert his vision into a reality. In this chapter, we'll elaborate on these three roles to show how you can use them to implement your vision in your own organization.

# THE LEADER AS SPOKESPERSON FOR THE VISION

A vision is little more than an empty dream until it is widely shared and accepted. Only then does it acquire the force necessary to change an organization and move it in the intended direction.

But how does a vision become widely shared? Leaders from Moses to Helmut Kohl, and everyone in between, have always known the answer. The key is connecting with people in a meaningful way to persuade them to change their perceptions about what is important for them and for the organization. For literally thousands of years, leaders, philosophers, scholars in rhetoric and linguistics, and lately the mass media have been exploring processes of persuasion using words and images. There is a vast literature on this subject, far too extensive to review here. However, according to one of the best of the recent books, if there is a single rule that governs change situations, it is that "unless people believe they have *chosen* to adopt a new attitude and behavior and feel rewarded, they are likely to revert to old ways" (Reardon, 1991, p. 210).

The key to gaining widespread commitment to a new vision, therefore, is to present the vision in such a way that people will want to participate and will freely choose to do so. This certainly cannot be done through coercion or manipulation, for people must freely and enthusiastically accept the vision or they will not have the energy or excitement to work for its fulfillment. Besides, the use of coercion or manipulation implies a cynical belief that people are reluctant participants in the work of the organization. The only approach that will work is based on exactly the opposite belief — that people are interested and active partners and colleagues in the enterprise — and involves discussing the vision with them in terms that address their own legitimate concerns and interests. This means connecting with people in a way that resonates with their own deepest feelings about what is right and worth doing. Kouzes and Posner (1987, p. 115) put it this way: "Leaders find that common thread that weaves together the fabric of human needs into a colorful tapestry. They seek out the brewing consensus among those they would lead. In order to do this, they develop a deep understanding of the collective yearnings. They listen carefully for quiet whisperings in dark corners. They attend to the subtle cues. They sniff the air to get the scent. They watch the faces. They get a sense of what people want, what they value, what they dream about."

So what leaders must do is form their intentions with full knowledge of the aspirations and values already extant in the organization and then merge the resulting vision with the existing mental framework of each individual stakeholder — workers and managers inside the organization, as well as customers, investors, and other important people outside the organization. Leaders accomplish this through the three main tasks of the leader as spokesperson: communication, networking, and what my colleague Warren Bennis calls "living the dream."

### Communication

Leaders communicate in many ways. In fact, it is hard for them *not* to communicate, for they are so closely watched, referred to, and emulated that whatever they do or say — and even what they don't do or don't say — communicates volumes to others. The only question, then, is what leaders choose to communicate and how they choose to do so.

Perhaps the most universal approach to communication is the simple dialogue, which some leaders have developed to a high art. Political leaders like Helmut Kohl are often masters at the one-on-one discussion. I'll never forget, as a young man, walking into the office of a vice-president at Univac looking for help with several problems and walking out a scant half hour later with no answers to my problems but a whole new agenda — his agenda — and feeling good about it! For years, I wondered how he did that. Now I see he did it by listening sympathetically to my story, sensing my desire to help the company, putting my concerns into a larger context — his overall vision for the division — and then sending me off to solve the problems myself. The remarkable thing is that he did it all so smoothly and sincerely that I came away feeling supported, encouraged, and excited about the future of the firm.

Other leaders communicate best through memoranda.

George Ball, the chairman of Prudential Bache Securities, sends a weekly memo to most of his 17,000 employees stressing a vision of that firm as a swift light cruiser on stormy seas outflanking the big battleships of Wall Street. His memos may get repetitious and may sometimes even be the brunt of office jokes, but they show passion and personal conviction, and they help people see what the vision means for their future and how it can help them.

Still other leaders are accomplished public speakers, able to convey positive and optimistic visions of the future purely through the often colorful spoken word. They are skilled at conjuring up dramatic images and conveying their own enthusiasm and passion for the vision to diverse audiences through humor, metaphors, and stories that capture the imagination and excitement of their listeners. Some dramatic examples include Abraham Lincoln's Gettysburg address, John Kennedy's speech at the Berlin Wall, and Martin Luther King's "I Have a Dream" speech.

Many leaders communicate the vision through a variety of other media, using letters or pamphlets to introduce the concept and then reinforcing it with posters, notices on bulletin boards, videotape presentations, and articles in house organs. They may disseminate the vision to outside audiences at the annual meeting or through letters, the annual report, press releases, interviews, or radio and television appearances. There is no lack of detailed information in the literature on techniques you can use to communicate vision (for recent examples, see Kouzes and Posner, 1987; Tregoe, Zimmerman, Smith, and Tobia, 1989; Pascarella and Frohman, 1989; Block, 1987).

### Networking

Effective leaders invest a good deal of their time in networking with people both inside and outside their organizations to generate trust and consensus for their visions. For example, Helmut Kohl could not have achieved his vision of

German reunification had he not carefully built up personal relationships with Soviet, American, and European leaders and then successfully lobbied and negotiated to gain their support. Nor could he have been successful without knowing exactly who to deal with inside the two Germanys and how to gain their commitment to the process, or at least their agreement not to oppose it.

All leaders must become advocates for the future of their organizations in a variety of settings: with boards of directors, groups of distributors, local governments, unions, regulatory agencies, suppliers, trade associations, and the investment community. As the spokesperson for the as-yet-unborn future, leaders hold out not only a hope and a dream but also a way to move forward, to achieve progress, and at the same time, to strengthen the organization's bonds with its constituents.

Effective leaders are good listeners, too. In network settings, the leader pays attention, hoping to discover and exploit common interests that can be consistently served by the organization with its new sense of direction. Feedback from others not only helps in the crucial tasks of implementing the vision but also alerts leaders to potential problems and provides early warning of environmental changes that may require alterations in the vision.

It may also be necessary to negotiate for resources in these settings or to offer concessions in exchange for commitment to the new direction. Effective leaders are usually skilled negotiators who can press their own views and reach agreements that advance the vision.

### Personifying the Vision

Martin Luther King knew he had to be the very embodiment of the civil rights movement if he expected to make a difference. On one occasion, he said, "People cannot become devoted to Christianity until they find Christ, to democracy until they find Lincoln and Jefferson and Roosevelt, to communism until they find Marx and Lenin and Stalin . . . people are often led to causes and often become committed to great ideas through persons who personify those ideas" (Bennett, 1964, p. 127).

In some of my classes, I ask students to interview corporate leaders about their philosophy. In various less eloquent ways, the leaders often concur with King's sentiments that the organization tends to take on the characteristics of its leader. One bank vice-president told a student that the leader must "walk what he talks." Another said, "If you don't stand for something, you'll fall for anything." The president of an electrical distributor said, "The vision becomes part of you. Then you start to represent the direction yourself, as well as try to keep it going."

Leaders live the vision by making all their actions and behaviors consistent with it and by creating a sense of urgency and passion for its attainment. You can do this in many ways, among them the following:

■ *How you make and honor commitments.* Integrity and consistency are important to any leader who seeks to be trusted, and without trust, there is little chance that a vision will be embraced by those whose commitment is essential for the vision to be realized. As Machiavelli once said, "Nothing makes a prince so much esteemed as the undertaking of great enterprises and the setting of a noble example in his own person."

■ *What you say in formal and especially informal settings.* Political figures, for example, know their every word will be minutely scrutinized by the press and opponents for evidence of hidden preferences, convictions, and values. In a corporate setting, every speech and meeting, no matter what the purpose, provides a setting within which leaders can reinforce the sense of commitment and urgency they feel for their vision.

■ *What you express interest in and what questions you ask.* Leaders often express passion for their agendas in the hope of exciting others to support their visions. However, even mildly expressed interest or curiosity will be noticed by colleagues and subordinates. For example, if the president of a computer software firm continually asks questions about the adequacy of documentation and freedom from errors of a new programming product, that conveys a strong message about quality and concern for the user that would not be expressed if his questions only related to sales and profits.

- *Where you choose to go and with whom you spend time.* Alfred P. Sloan, the great president of General Motors, spent much of his time visiting auto dealers, which not only provided him with invaluable firsthand information about the car market but also elevated the importance of the dealers throughout the General Motors hierarchy.

- *When you choose to act and how you make your actions known.* Timing is always important, but no less important is the way actions are taken, including who is consulted in the process, who is brought in to share responsibility or glory, where the action takes place, in what sequence, and so forth.

- *How you organize your staff and your physical surroundings.* An executive whose vision is for her organization to be the low-cost leader in the industry, for example, would do well to set an example with a modest office for herself, a small staff, eating in the company cafeteria, traveling coach rather than first class, and so forth.

The spokesperson task is not complete until everyone in the organization and all the major external stakeholders viscerally understand where the organization is headed and have a high degree of shared commitment to the vision. They must also have a sense of urgency for the vision. There are always crises of the moment that seem more compelling; solving them will have a measurable impact on current performance and, in many cases, on bonuses, promotions, or other forms of imminent reward. Sometimes the vision adds its own collection of problems to the already crowded list of existing crises. Helping people rise above these pressures and keeping everyone's attention focused on the longer-term vision are additional challenges for you as spokesperson.

Once the vision is accepted and there is a shared perception of its urgency, the leader can move on to the change agent role.

# THE LEADER AS CHANGE AGENT FOR THE VISION

The leader's purpose as a change agent is to make the investment decisions and other organizational changes necessary to realize the vision. When a visionary leader has an extraordinary ability to act in this role, he or she literally creates the future and, in the process, also changes the way we think about it. For example, Walt Disney almost single-handedly reinvented the idea of an amusement park, Betty Friedan reconceptualized the role of women in society, and Ted Turner completely altered the role of cable television in the home. They all started with a powerful vision, of course, but then were able to marshal the resources and organize their constituencies to make it happen.

Change is, of course, a constant or perhaps even accelerating condition of today's corporations. Tom Peters, in his best-seller *Thriving on Chaos*, thinks that "the world has not just turned upside down. It is turning every which way at an accelerating pace. . . . Today, loving change, tumult, even chaos is a prerequisite for survival, let alone success" (1987, p. 45). Into this stewing, turbulent brew comes the visionary leader trying to steer the changes in the direction of the vision, a job that might be likened to retargeting a space station long after its launch.

As a leader, you are likely to have the skills and authority to both directly and indirectly steer the changes. Directly, you have the authority to make the key decisions on resource allocations, staffing, structures, information flows, and operating processes that determine what shall or shall not be done by the organization. Indirectly, you can influence the behavior of others and orient them toward the new destination through consultation, participation, persuasion, inspiration, and rewards. In addition, you can set up special task forces charged with specific implementation responsibilities.

Both directly and indirectly, you can work to develop strategic thinking supportive of your vision and alter the organizational climate to make the vision's attainment more likely.

### Thinking Strategically

Knowing where the organization should be headed is one thing; developing a strategy for getting there is quite another. Ted Turner had a vision of dominating the field of competitive sailing. He then had to develop a strategy to win the America's Cup: design a world-class competitive boat, pick a crew, train them, select races in which to compete, and so forth.

One of the early strategic decisions you must make is whether to pursue the vision alone or to seek strategic alliances. Few organizations these days can undertake dramatic changes without outside help. Even giant IBM, with all its resources and innovative capacity, has found it necessary to build strategic alliances with other strong domestic and foreign firms to retain and build its competitive position. If you make the decision to collaborate with outside organizations, there are many possibilties, ranging from investments and joint ventures to partnerships and mergers.

Another strategic decision you must make is your choice of goals and objectives—that is, what you intend to be accomplished and when. For an organization like a community hospital, the vision might be to become the preeminent family care facility in its metropolitan region, a goal might be to build a separate wing of the hospital for maternity cases, and an objective might be to increase the number of maternity cases by 10 percent per year for the next five years.

In a small organization, the leader will likely be the one to set the goals and objectives, perhaps with input from staff or line personnel. In larger organizations, it is the leader's job to see that the goals and objectives are established by others, perhaps reserving approval authority to verify their consistency with the vision. In some of the best-managed companies, the responsibility for setting goals and objectives is widely dispersed, sometimes reaching right down to the workers on the production line.

As a leader, you also make (or recommend to a board of directors) the strategic investment decisions committing resources to new facilities, locations, and equipment as needed to accomplish your vision. You must also be sure there is a sufficient capital base to accomplish the vision. Organizations have many types of capital they can deploy in achieving a new vision, only some of which appear on a traditional balance sheet. The most obvious is physical capital: the sum total of all the cash, facilities, tools and equipment, borrowing capacity, and similar hard assets that can be diverted to the job of implementing the new vision. Leaders can raise physical capital (for example, through borrowing, stock offerings, fund raising, and the like) and typically have full authority to allocate it, or at least to approve its uses. This is perhaps the most common and direct way a leader can establish priorities and institutionalize a new agenda.

Another widely recognized type of capital is human capital, consisting of all the skills, talents, experience, technological know-how, and capabilities of workers and managers in the organization. The visionary leader builds human capital mainly through decisions on hiring, staffing, and training. When the president of IBM shifts employees from the large computer division to personal computers and from programming tasks to customer service, he is making a massive commitment to implementing a new vision for IBM.

The most subtle, often underappreciated, form of capital is organizational capital, the nonphysical and nonhuman assets that enable the organization to do things that would be impossible for others or would take years to accomplish. One of these assets is the organization's reputation, which is another way of saying the trust and confidence of the organization's major constituencies. Sometimes reputation is encapsulated in a brand name or symbol—for example, Mercedes Benz or the Red Cross—that has earned so much status from years of quality and high performance that people will trust the organization when it announces it is moving off in a new direction.

There are other forms of organizational capital as well. The technology, traditions, and team training of the U.S. Marines represent a national investment in an organization to deal effectively with any new military challenge anywhere in the world at short notice. The research and development capacity of Merck is a formidable asset that enables it to take the product initiative in many new pharmaceutical areas. The ubiquitous nature of its reservations system allowed American Airlines to introduce new route structures and services with instant accessibility much faster than its competitors. The favorable location of a community hospital, the unique readership of a newspaper or magazine, the universal acceptance of a bank's credit card, the distinctive art collection of the British Museum, and Disney's film library are all examples of organizational capital accumulated over many years that may not appear or may be grossly undervalued on a balance sheet but nevertheless represent tremendous assets in implementing vision.

Finally, be sure the strategic thinking guided by your vision permeates the organization from top to bottom and actually guides decision making. This does not mean you should revive the rigid (and often ignored) formal strategic planning processes so much in fashion in the 1970s, but rather that normal operating decisions should be taken with a strategic perspective — that is, with a broad long-term perspective that moves the organization in the direction of the vision.

With strategic alliances, goals, and objectives, the three forms of capital, and strategic thinking throughout the organization, you will have established a necessary framework within which organizational change can take place.

### Altering the Organizational Climate

The organizational climate consists of the structures, processes, and culture that collectively determine how the organization functions. The visionary leader must overcome resistance to change and adapt the organizational climate to the new agenda.

Organizations tend to seek stability and resist change, especially change as dramatic and pervasive as a new direction. After all, the new vision may complicate life for many people in the organization. It may affect or alter working relationships that have taken years to build. It may reduce the power or influence of some current managers and departments while creating new managers and departments with new functions and responsibilities. It may rechannel information and resources or perhaps lead to wholesale relocations, even terminations.

People are comfortable with the familiar and fear the unknown, often with good reason. Still, there are things you can do to overcome resistance to change:

■ You can implement the new visions deliberately, making sure everyone understands the new direction and introducing the least disruptive or threatening changes first. When Frances Hesselbein decided to reorient the Girl Scouts from traditional interests like sewing and household skills to activities reflecting a society with bold new opportunities for women in science, business, and the environment, she moved deliberately but steadily within the established culture, introducing new merit badges, updating the uniform and the *Girl Scout Handbook,* training a new cadre of volunteers, reaching out to new membership in the inner cities, and ultimately changing the way the organization thought about itself.

■   In some cases, you can avoid resistance by isolating the units responsible for pioneering the new direction from the existing organization until they prove their worth or acquire legitimacy and acceptance. IBM did this with its PC project, and so did Honda with its Acura car and General Motors with the Saturn project.

■   You can put the new thrust in the hands of younger people with less commitment to the status quo and extend it later to other parts of the organization. Or you can assign responsibilities to opinion leaders and champions in the organization who know how to take advantage of informal networks to establish a sense of renewal and progress with the new vision. In his Pulitzer Prize–winning book *The Soul of a New Machine,* Tracy Kidder showed why some people are willing to take on the risk and challenge of a new direction when he quoted one champion as saying: "I guess the reason I do it fundamentally is that there's a certain satisfaction in building a machine like this, which is important to the company, which is on its way to becoming a billion dollar company. There aren't that many opportunities in this world to be where the action is, making an impact. . . . I was looking for opportunity, responsibility, visibility. . . . I wanted to see what I was worth" (1981, p. 143). Such a champion develops an enthusiasm and vested interest in the new vision that infect others. This helps to persuade them to "sign up" and, in turn, become missionaries for the message.

■   You can foster a culture that embraces change and innovation, so that the new vision is not seen as something unusual but rather as part of the continuing evolution of your organization. In a company like Sony, for example, change is so frequent, so highly valued and nourished, that even a radical change like the acquisition of CBS records and Columbia Pictures is taken more or less in stride.

But even a total victory over the forces opposing change is only a first step in constructing the proper organizational climate for the new vision. There are many decisions to be made, of which the following may be among the most pivotal in reshaping the climate:

*1.  What values are most consistent with the new vision?* Every vision calls for certain values. A military vision like restoring the government of Kuwait requires loyalty, discipline, patriotism, self-sacrifice, and determination. A new vision for a hospital may require the values of human service, caring, sensitivity, and respect for physician skills, scientific findings, and human dignity. Trust and integrity are indispensable values for implementing any change, especially a new vision.

Values tend to persist in an organization. However, there are often many values present at any given time, some of them contradictory or repressed. For example, people may value both individuality and conformance to organizational norms, both competitive prowess and cooperative behavior, both ambition and unselfishness, both stability and change. The very act of stating a new vision gives voice and strength to some values that are already present and tends to make other values seem less appropriate.

Moreover, while it is difficult to alter values, it is not impossible. One way to do so is by recognizing and rewarding displays of values more consistent with the vision. Another is by insisting that all managers adhere to a lofty credo that reflects a desired set of values, an approach that has proved especially effective at companies like Johnson & Johnson and Ben and Jerry's Ice Cream. Still another approach is to hire and promote people who already have the appropriate values.

**2. How shall performance in support of the vision be encouraged, recognized, and rewarded?**

It is well known that behavior that is rewarded is usually the behavior that organizations get, whether the rewards are purely economic, like salary increases and bonuses, or largely psychosocial, like recognition, approval, and status. Most rewards tend to be for short-term performance and in response to financially oriented information. Instead, progress toward a new vision is likely to require attention to longer-term matters, sometimes at the expense of short-term performance. Furthermore, vision-oriented activities tend to be measurable less in terms of financial data than in such qualitative measures as customer satisfaction, new product innovation, and growth of competitive strength. Selecting the best measures and tying them to reward systems are important steps you must take in orienting behavior toward your vision.

**3. What are the best ways to organize for the vision?**

Most new visions require some changes in the existing organizational structures. An organization designed for a future as a low-cost producer will likely be lean, vertically integrated, and oriented to efficiency and quality. An organization designed for innovation, on the other hand, is likely to be flatter, more flexible, and more collegial. The key is to design an organization that fits the vision and maps most directly onto the major customers and constituencies to be served.

**4. What new operating policies or processes should you develop to move toward the vision?**

When AT&T had to transform itself from a giant government-regulated monopoly to a competitive telephone company, it developed a whole range of new operating policies and completely restructured its operations, spinning off the Bell operating companies, for example. As a minimum, most organizations find that new visions require new information systems and new patterns of communication and decision making. In addition, it is a rare new vision that does not require a reformulation of operations and a revision of policies to conform with the new direction. You have the responsibility to initiate and approve such changes and then to keep an eye on them to be sure they are accomplishing your purpose.

*5.   What additional skills are needed, and should they be developed internally through development and training or hired from the outside?*

Few organizations have all the skills on board to shift in a new direction. Even the giant General Motors Corporation, when faced with the need to modernize its cars and include more in the way of electronic hardware and software, found itself deficient and decided to acquire Hughes and Electronic Data Systems. New skills can be developed internally, of course, and in-house training is already a multibillion dollar business in the United States. But internal development takes time and money and may disrupt present operations. Hiring from the outside is quicker but costlier, especially since the new hire has much to learn about the organizational culture and may take months or years to adapt.

There is much more that can be said about your activities in the change agent role, modifying organizational behavior through new strategies and organizational climates. Fortunately, this is a subject well covered in the management literature, and much help is available, perhaps even from your own internal staff. Once these changes are in place your most critical leadership role shifts to coaching.

# THE LEADER AS COACH FOR THE VISION

The coaching role concerns your relationship to followers. Your main purpose as coach is to empower people to act in the name of the new vision and to help sustain their commitment to it.

Leaders tend to take their coaching role quite seriously. When George Bush took office as president, he issued the following memorandum of understanding to his staff: "Think big. Challenge the system. Adhere to the highest ethical standards. Be on the record as much as possible. Be frank. Fight hard for your position. When I make a call, we move as a team. Work with Congress. Represent the United States with dignity" (Safire, 1990, p. 31).

Some coaching can take place one on one, as, for example, when you act as mentor or teacher commenting on or celebrating an individual's accomplishments, attempting to correct a misperception, or helping to resolve a conflict. In such interactions, the organizational behavior literature suggests that subordinate satisfaction with leaders is more likely for leaders "who act friendly, open, sympathetic, and helpful toward subordinates, treat them fairly, show respect, demonstrate concern for their needs and feelings, and do things to advance their careers. . . . [while also] providing recognition and equitable rewards, representing subordinate interests in relations with people outside of the work unit, and allowing participation in making decisions when appropriate" (Yukl, 1989, p. 275).

In a real organization of any size, however, the amount of time that a leader can devote to any single individual is quite limited. For example, even in an organization as small as a professional football team, the coach has so many responsibilities—picking the lineup, designing plays, developing game strategies, working with the front office, reviewing scouting reports, meeting with reporters, coordinating the assistant coaches, and so forth—that at best, he can spend only a limited amount of time with any individual player. By the time an organization reaches even the size of a symphony orchestra, there is no alternative but for the leader/conductor to assume that each individual is totally competent in playing his or her part and to concentrate nearly all coaching efforts on the group as an ensemble.

In practical terms, therefore, coaching with regard to vision deals with larger organizational units than the individual. While people come into organizations as individuals, they do most of their work in teams — that is, groups of people clustered around task assignments. The team or work group thus becomes a critical element in implementing vision.

This is not to say that the individual is unimportant. On the contrary, it is only through the individual's commitment and energy that the desired vision will be achieved. However, this commitment and energy is exercised within an institutional and social context that strongly influences the level of achievement. The context links individuals to others and to the larger organization and society, thereby allowing workers to see themselves as part of a larger undertaking, which enhances their status and self-esteem. The context provides material and emotional support for individuals, defining the meaning and value of their individual work. It offers a setting within which learning and personal growth can be experienced, measured, and appreciated. The context also provides memory, rituals, values, tools, and structure for the work of both the group and the individual. It promotes cooperation, mutual trust, and teamwork, emphasizing common interests, encouraging sharing of information, and providing mechanisms for resolving conflicts.

You can shape the social contexts in your organization in many ways to suit your vision, especially through your decisions and commitments about the following:

- *Who you choose to assign to groups and tasks.* Visionary leaders know that people must be selected for critical and sensitive assignments not just for their technical skills but also on the basis of their dedication to the vision, their ability to work well with others, and their track record in getting things done. IBM's special work group on the personal computer, for example, contained not just some of the best technical people available but also those most committed to the ideal of an affordable, quickly available desktop computer.

- *The amount and types of resources and support services you make available to work groups.* Teams that are most concerned with the vision should have freer and quicker access to money, special skills, equipment, and other resources that may be in short supply in the organization.

- *The design of incentive systems.* Your choice of who and what is rewarded greatly influences the way groups work and their loyalty to the vision. In the Ford Motor Company, for example, with their recent emphasis on "quality is job one," rewards are strongly keyed to quality improvements.

- *The way jobs are structured and allocated among work groups.* A consumer products corporation with a vision of innovation and rapid market response, for example, should structure many jobs to facilitate market feedback and should allocate major responsibilities like pricing and product design to marketing research teams or brand managers who are in the best position to understand customer needs and wants.

- *Your choice of people to head the teams.* The leaders of work groups should be chosen for their ability to mobilize activity toward achieving your vision. Sometimes this can best be done by unconventional or counterintuitive assignments, for example, assigning a software expert to head a computer design team or making the inventor of a new product an internal champion to see that it is marketed and serviced properly.

- *The goals and expectations you associate with each organizational unit.* Visionary leaders point the way for the entire organization and are the most influential voices in setting goals and expectations. When President John Kennedy told N.A.S.A. to put a man on the moon by 1970, his directive established not only a compelling vision of leadership in space but also led to a series of subordinate goals and expectations that had to be fulfilled to achieve the overall vision — a fuels breakthrough by a certain time, selection and training of the astronauts, and so forth.

To illustrate how all this comes together, consider how Volvo, the Swedish automobile manufacturer, went about reorienting its operating style to implement a vision of much greater customer responsiveness. In its plant at Uddevalla, Sweden, the company set up work teams with complete responsibility for building a car. These teams were authorized to accept customer's orders, work directly with dealers, and even to follow a car throughout its life cycle by getting customer feedback and quality and maintenance reports on the vehicle. Individuals were chosen for their ability to work together and were evaluated as a team. They were given all necessary resources, including information and access to customers and dealers. Their goals and expectations were designed to be customer driven, and they were given considerable freedom and flexibility on how to accomplish them.

Thus, by establishing the team contexts, you can create communities of interest around your vision statement and give the vision meaning and substance. This is important because people are constantly seeking meaning in their work. They want to know why the organization is doing what it does, how it will benefit them and others, and where they and their contributions fit into the grand scheme of things.

Moreover, most people find personal fulfillment in working with others for a worthwhile purpose, and it is precisely such a purpose that your vision supplies and the context supports. Together, the vision and the contexts help to direct the energies of the people toward a common end, to build a shared commitment to the vision, and to empower people to act to make its attainment possible.

## LEADING FROM THE MIDDLE

Most of the ideas in this chapter apply equally well whether you are a top executive or are leading a unit at a lower level in a large organization. However, those at middle or lower levels face additional problems and challenges in implementing their visions that leaders at the top, by virtue of the wide scope of their authority, seldom encounter.

At the outset, let's acknowledge that leadership — not management, but true leadership — is vitally needed throughout all levels of modern organizations. Today's highly charged, turbulent environments impinge on an organization at thousands of points in ever changing ways, requiring long-term as well as immediate responses at every level. To cope, many organizations have transformed themselves from slowly moving monoliths into large, pulsating agglomerations of smaller businesses, each targeted to specific products, services, markets, or geographical areas and each led by a person with considerable clout and decision-making freedom to set direction and navigate his or her unit through the unique conditions confronting it. Large organizations could hardly do otherwise, for as Harold Leavitt points out, "These days no CEO, even the brilliant founder, and no R&D group can generate all of the adventurous explorations, large and small, that organizations need to maintain their vitality" (1986, p. 126).

Top executives in most successful organizations readily acknowledge how dependent they are on midlevel leaders. They put their trust in them to make the right decisions, delegate ample authority to allow them to operate and build their organizations with considerable freedom and flexibility, and support them with necessary training and resources. As a result, these midlevel leaders have no less need for vision than the leaders to whom they report, and they too must be spokespersons, change agents, and coaches for their own visions.

The visions of midlevel executives must support, or at least not conflict with, those at a higher level. In practice, this is not as restrictive as it may seem. Recall the Prime Pet Foods example in Part Two, where the new direction called for innovation in high-quality pet food and health products. This points the entire division in a particular direction but does not preclude a midlevel leader designing a separate vision for his or her unit that may focus on the southeastern U.S. market or on vitamins for cats or on a line of food products for show dogs. In fact, a new direction should inspire a midlevel leader to seek new opportunities.

A common hazard reported by some midlevel executives is that they are treated like managers, not leaders — that is, they feel under so much pressure for efficiency and short-term performance they are unable to pay attention to longer-range issues like developing a vision or building the unit for the future. Managers can be leaders as well, but only if they have enough time to devote to both responsibilities.

If you find yourself in this situation, acknowledge the pressure but don't allow it to monopolize your attention. Instead, take the initiative. Delegate as much of your day-to-day responsibilities as you can to subordinates to free up time for your leadership roles. Build teamwork and empower your people to make decisions by letting them know that you trust them and will back them up. Then, pay more attention to longer-term matters. Collect information on the changing environments that affect your unit. Look for emerging threats and opportunities. Keep asking yourself and others why things are being done in a certain way and how they could be improved. Enlist others in your search for new directions.

As you become more of a visionary leader, make your superiors allies in your effort. Peter Block, a perceptive consultant in organizational development, suggests that you imagine your unit to be a separate business, for which you have full responsibility, and try to cast your boss in the role of banker or board member. In either role, the boss would have a respected voice in your choice of direction and would exercise final approval of investments and strategies, but you are still the acknowledged leader. You are "the architect of the organization, choosing its form and future . . . not just a laborer, following another's plans" (Block, 1987, p. 195).

# THE FORMULA FOR VISIONARY LEADERSHIP

By this point, it should be obvious that there is no single thing you can do to "make it happen"—that is, to ensure that your vision is successfully implemented. Communication alone won't do it, no matter how eloquent and persuasive you are. Organizational changes alone won't do it, no matter how appropriate they may be or how great an impact they have on the organization. Effective individual participation or teamwork alone won't do it either, no matter how competent or well supported. But all these together, when informed by a vision that meets the criteria laid out in the earlier chapters, can make the difference.

The relationships are clear:

**Vision + Communication = Shared Purpose**

**Shared Purpose + Empowered People + Appropriate Organizational Changes + Strategic Thinking = Successful Visionary Leadership**

When Walt Disney said, "If you can dream it, you can do it," this is what he meant.

# CHAPTER 8

# Running a Race with No End:
## The Re-Visioning Process

The heights by great men reached and kept
Were not attained by sudden flight,
But they, while their companions slept,
Were toiling upward in the night.
        —HENRY WADSWORTH LONGFELLOW

Nothing is more common than a vision that has over-stayed its welcome. Every leader wants an enduring vision, so once the organization is committed to it, all energies can be invested in its fulfillment. But although a vision may be the right one at the time it is formulated, rarely is it right for all time. The world changes, and so must the vision. Even great visionary leaders sometimes feel themselves at the mercy of change. Napoleon, for example, who must surely have been one of the great visionary leaders of all time, once said the following: "I have conceived of many plans, but I was never free to execute one of them. For all that I held the rudder, and with a strong hand, the waves were always a good deal stronger. I was never in truth my own master; I was always governed by circumstance" (Durant and Durant, 1975, p. 241).

Or consider the following more contemporary examples:

- Edwin H. Land built the Polaroid Company on a successful vision of an instantly developing film. However, when he tried to extend the vision to Polavision, an instant movie system, the company lost over $250 million. By then, video recorders had arrived and the home movie market virtually disappeared.

■ Sebastian Kresge had a vision at the turn of the century of a chain of variety stores offering very low prices made possible by large-scale centralized control and purchasing. It was an excellent vision that brought prosperity until the early 1950s, when shopping centers, supermarkets, and large drug chains began to attract large numbers of the customers who used to buy at Kresge's. A new vision was formulated that led to the K-Mart chain of discount department stores, which were such a great success that by 1976, Kresge was second only to Sears in general merchandising. But soon enough, that vision was also challenged by a wave of specialty retailers, warehouse clubs, and regional discount chains like Wal-Mart that better met the needs of their local customers.

■ Whole industries can be destroyed or completely reoriented by changes beyond their control. For example, environmental regulations virtually eliminated the asbestos industry, medical research forced cigarette companies to diversify, and international competition crowded out U.S. television and steel manufacturers.

An important part of the art of visionary leadership, therefore, lies in monitoring change, making the necessary midcourse corrections, and knowing when to initiate a new vision-forming process. Thus, far from being the last word, a vision is part of a continuing process of orienting the organization to the emerging realities of the outside world. This is best done by fostering organizational learning.

# ORGANIZATIONAL LEARNING

Sony is a learning organization. It learns from its highly regarded research staff, from its production workers, sales staff, engineers, and managers. It learns from people outside the corporation, too—from its customers and dealers, from its major suppliers, from scientists at universities, securities analysts, industry publications, and professional conferences and trade fairs around the world. The learning takes place not just at the top but at every level in the organization. Learning is everybody's business, and the result is one of the most innovative and visionary companies in the world. We know that people learn, but how does an organization learn, and what role does vision play in the process?

In a short, brilliant work called *No Limits to Learning*, an important distinction is made between maintenance learning, which is learning designed to maintain an organization by increasing its ability to deal with known and recurring problems, and innovative learning, which is "the type of learning that can bring change, renewal, restructuring and problem reformulation" (Botkin, Elmandjra, and Malitza, 1979, p. 10).

In the case of vision, maintenance learning is involved as the entire organization absorbs the vision into its ethos, its ideology, its very raison d'être and then makes minor adaptations to changing conditions while still moving in the desired direction. Innovative learning helps leaders recognize the need for a totally new direction when the old vision is no longer effective. Both types of organizational learning are needed, the first for adaptation, the second for renewal.

Organizational learning is facilitated when there is openness and mutual trust that allow people to embrace change and experimentation without feeling personally threatened. It also helps if the culture supports widespread participation in decision making, an entrepreneurial ethic, and a diversity of skills and viewpoints. But most of all, a learning organization needs plenty of feedback, which can only be obtained through careful monitoring and tracking of the vision.

### Monitoring and Tracking the Vision

Monitoring involves gathering information about how well the vision is being implemented in the organization and measuring the organization's progress in achieving the new direction. Some key questions to be answered are the following:

- How well is the organization doing in moving in the desired direction? Are there enough changes being made, and is the rate of progress satisfactory?

- Are people committed to the vision, acting as if it were their own, and willing to take the initiative and incur prudent risks to achieve the vision?

- Are the goals and priorities of organizational units, as well as of new projects and program proposals, consistent with the vision? Have new options opened up?

- Are the organization's structures, processes, plans, reward systems, and policies consistent with the vision?

- Do people feel they are pushing the boundaries of their field, that they are "where the action is"? Are they optimistic and enthusiastic about the prospects for the organization?

- Are people communicating and cooperating with each other in the accomplishment of the vision, and are they being recognized for their participation in such activities?

- Are influential managers championing the vision, and is there evidence of confidence in the leadership?

- Is the culture supportive of the vision or moving in that direction?

- Has the organization been innovative enough in implementing the vision?

The information required to answer these questions is available from many sources: direct observation and measurement, attentive listening, informal conversations and rap sessions, performance reports, plans and programs, accounting data, task forces, and surveys, to mention just a few.

While monitoring is mostly an internally directed activity, tracking involves gathering information about the effectiveness of the vision in the external environment, including assessing changes in the environment that may suggest the need for an organizational response or perhaps even re-visioning. Some key questions to be answered include the following:

- Do all the external stakeholders in the organization, especially customers, suppliers, and shareholders, understand and support the vision? Do they view it favorably?

- Is the vision accomplishing its purpose in terms of the organization's measures of effectiveness? For example, are trends in market share, customer satisfaction, and public relations as favorable as expected with the new vision?

- How is the marketplace changing in ways significant for the organization's sense of direction? Specifically, are there new threats or opportunities surfacing among peer organizations and competitors or among clients and customers?

- How is the external environment changing in ways significant for the organization's sense of direction? Specifically, are there new threats or opportunities surfacing in the social, economic, political, and technological environments that could affect the viability of the vision statement?

- How does the image of the products or services of the organization compare in terms of relative value to those of other organizations?

- Are there alternative visions being employed by other organizations that should be tracked and studied for the insights they might offer?

Some organizations establish rather formal environmental scanning systems to continually collect answers to questions like these. For example, the Trend Analysis Program of the American Council of Life Insurance regularly scans newspapers, magazines, and professional and technical publications to track information that may have relevance for future products, services, or strategies of companies in that industry. Other organizations use less formal means, including networking with a wide range of outside individuals, subscribing to key publications, conducting polls and surveys of key stakeholders, inviting outside speakers to address executives from time to time, and using expert consultants when issues or trends appear to be especially relevant to the organization's vision.

### Revising the Vision

There is no regular schedule for revising a vision. As long as a vision appears to be working and is consistent with developments in the internal and external environments, it should be affirmed and supported. At some point, however, signals from the monitoring and tracking activities may suggest the need for altering or perhaps even replacing the vision, as illustrated below:

- Bank of America, long one of the strongest banks in the country, sees that its major competitors are not other American banks but rather the strongest Japanese and European banks, who are collecting deposits and moving capital rapidly around the world to take advantage of the most attractive lending opportunities, wherever they are. The result: Bank of America merges with Security Pacific National Bank, its largest regional competitor, to achieve economies of scale and gain international clout. Now, how should Citicorp revise its vision in light of this merger?

- IBM, long the major force in the computer business, sees that its bread-and-butter product line, large computers, no longer has the growth potential it once did, while the rapidly growing personal computer and work station markets are being attacked on all fronts by strong, innovative competitors. The result: IBM does the previously unthinkable; it forms a joint venture with archrival Apple Computer, Inc., to unify the standards for personal computers and improve their user friendliness. Now, what should COMPAQ Computer do to revise its vision?

- The Atlantic Richfield Company, a well-managed integrated oil company marketing mainly in the western United States, sees that air pollution is getting so bad in major cities that regulators are moving to limit gasoline-driven cars and promote electric- or methane-propelled vehicles. The result: Atlantic Richfield devises a new vision of a low-emissions gasoline and moves out in front of the industry to advocate its use, gaining an enormous competitive advantage and public goodwill. Now what should Exxon do to revise its vision?

In these three examples, the companies were stimulated to develop new visions by external challenges likely to threaten their traditional operations in the future. These companies did not wait until it was too late—as the automobile companies appear to be doing—but chose to act as soon as the pattern became clear and while they still had wide latitude for action and investor support for innovative new directions. Their actions were boldly executed, well communicated, and welcomed by most of their stakeholders, especially investors, who promptly bid up their share prices. These new visions, in turn, necessitate re-visioning on the part of their competitors if they wish to avoid the risk of being left far behind.

There are no hard and fast rules for when you need to revise an existing vision. In Chapter One, some internal clues were identified, and in this chapter, some external signals worth watching for were added to the list. But a wise leader doesn't wait for the alert to be sounded before thinking of alternative new directions. Rather, the vision-forming process should be a continual one. You should be constantly developing and examining alternatives for change so that when and if the alert is sounded, you are prepared to act. In the cases of Bank of America, IBM, and Atlantic Richfield, the announcements of their new directions were dramatic and unexpected by the general public, but the directions most certainly had been contemplated and thoroughly explored by the leadership of the respective firms much earlier.

One way to be sure vision formation is a continuous process is by spreading the leadership role throughout your organization at every level, so that every unit is encouraged to develop its own vision.

# SPREADING VISIONARY LEADERSHIP

Minnesota Mining and Manufacturing, also known as 3M, is widely regarded as one of the most innovative companies in the world. In a typical year, more than one-third of its sales comes from products introduced within the preceding five years. The company is fairly bursting at the seams with leadership because any manager or employee who comes up with a new product idea is encouraged to lead the product development and marketing effort for that product. With over sixty thousand products, this creates lots of leadership opportunities, with each leader having to develop and achieve a unique vision.

The 3M company is not alone. Johnson & Johnson has a similar philosophy, forming relatively autonomous companies out of spinoffs from existing divisions. McDonald's and other franchisers have thousands of leader/entrepreneurs running their local outlets. Many corporations now consciously create and empower so-called "intrapreneurs" to find new market needs and fill them. They also encourage and support innovators who can create new products and find markets for them. Through such efforts, organizations hope to create product champions to lead their business development activities, but all of these roles—intrapreneur, innovator, and product champion—are just visionary leaders by other names.

Even in organizations less buffeted by free market pressures, there are thousands of potential roles for visionary leaders. A large university may have seventy or more department heads, each a potential visionary leader responsible for taking his or her unit to the frontier of a particular academic discipline and keeping it there. A government agency may have dozens of local offices, each headed by a leader who is in a position to create a vision for the future of that unit. Volunteer organizations like the Boy Scouts and United Way have room for thousands of visionary leaders at the local level to take charge, dream dreams, and build unique futures for their units.

So vision is possible—indeed, it is necessary—at many levels of an organization. Wherever leaders have control of some resources, accept responsibility for some activities, and are committed to making a difference, they should be mandated to develop an agenda and a sense of direction for their units consistent with the overall vision of the organization. In fact, whether they are required to do so or not, they should fervently *desire* to do so, for as one writer has said, "We claim ownership over our lives when we identify the future that we want for ourselves and our unit. Our deepest commitment is to choose to live, to choose the destiny that has been handed to us, and to choose to pursue that destiny. These choices are expressed at work when we create a vision for our unit and decide to pursue that vision at all costs" (Block, 1987, p. 83).

Visionary leaders at any level take ownership of their units by forming and committing to a meaningful vision, one that is important to the organization and its stakeholders and that promises to achieve something worthwhile. Such a vision becomes a magnet around which other people cluster and an infectious source of optimism and enthusiasm for all who work in the unit.

Leaders should be selected above all for their ability to form and implement such visions for their units. Perhaps the best indicator of such skill is a demonstrated record of successfully taking charge and pointing the way in some other setting—if not in another similar organization then whatever organization, public or private, the applicant has been associated with, for example, the military, a sports team, a college magazine, or a church group.

Such people are not docile conformists. They likely won't fit your normal hiring patterns. When you look for a visionary leader, don't look for a competent and experienced manager. Instead look for a budding Ted Turner, an H. Ross Perot, or a Wayne Huizenga, people who may appear to some as intelligent misfits, idiosyncratic and self-motivated, but who have the curiosity, drive, and ambition to want to change the world.

Once an individual has been selected for a leadership position, you can enhance his or her vision-forming skills with well-designed training and development programs. People can be put in positions where they observe other visionary leaders in action or where they are mentored by such individuals. A less direct approach includes studying the visions of great leaders, grappling with case materials, and reading broadly to better understand long-term trends and forecasts.

So the best way to ensure that the vision-forming process is alive and well—and continuously practiced—in your organization is to multiply the number of visionary leaders at all levels. Encourage them all to articulate visions worthy of their commitment and the organization's confidence. Applaud their initiative and tolerate their mistakes. The continuous visioning this stimulates will keep the process of organizational evolution alive and vital and will make it far less likely that important threats or opportunities will be overlooked. Moreover, the experience gained through continuous visioning will prove invaluable as these leaders are promoted into more responsible, higher-level leadership positions.

With the proliferation of visionary leadership at all levels, a leader at the top becomes what my colleague James O'Toole calls a leader of leaders. Not for him the image of a leader as shepherd and followers as sheep, dutifully following instructions. Instead, in a pattern now common in innovative companies, the "followers" are themselves leaders and are as qualified professionally as the leaders to whom they report. For those top executives who lead the leaders, vision is the sine qua non without which there could be no common framework and hence no collaboration, no mutual trust, and no hope of organizational progress. Like the Indian scout guiding the cavalry captains, you can lead only by getting out front and showing the way, keeping one eye firmly on the distant horizon and the other looking ahead to avoid traps along the path.

---

# THE PRUDENT VISIONARY

Not all visions turn out as well as hoped for. Some are derailed by unexpected events, much as the visions of the Emir of Kuwait for the future of his country collapsed when the Iraqis attacked. Some are just plain wrong to start with, as were the Marxist-Leninist visions of a workers' paradise in the Soviet Union. Some are as shortsighted as the visions of the auto companies focused on the next model year instead of on the next generation of vehicles. Some may be right for their organizations but are poorly implemented. And some are simply retained too long, growing as rusty and outdated as World War II radar in an era of satellite photography.

How can these and other failures of vision be avoided? Here are some suggestions to help you act as a prudent visionary:

1.   **Don't do it alone.** If you isolate yourself and hope to present your vision to the organization like Moses descending from Mount Sinai, you are simply asking for skepticism and resistance. Besides, you will have missed much that can be

learned from colleagues and others about trends and developments in the outside world and about what would be considered attractive or acceptable to various constituencies. After all, excellent proposals for the vision statement may already exist among the more farsighted members of your organization. By soliciting those suggestions and promoting wide participation in the search for a vision, you are preparing the organization for changes to come and possibly disarming those who would resist them.

There are many ways to avoid isolation. Many leaders, on assuming office, wisely poll their colleagues on what they think should be done to improve the prospects for the organization. You can set up a vision task force of influential and farsighted people and give them information collection and advisory responsibility on long-term directions. The Council of Economic Advisors once had such a role in the federal government until it degenerated into an advocacy committee for the incumbent president. You could also conduct a retreat, something similar to a QUEST session (Nanus, 1989), with a dozen or two top advisers to explore and discuss alternative future possibilities. One corporate CEO sends a list of questions— such as what the firm needs to do to become a great company, what key matters the CEO needs to focus on, and what the competition might do that requires preparation or response— to senior managers prior to their performance reviews and asks them to be prepared to discuss such matters (DePree, 1989).

2. *Don't be overly idealistic.* A vision should represent a worthwhile challenge, but it loses its force if people think it is too ambitious or unrealistic. When Soviet leaders claimed that the Soviet Union would bury the United States economically, the Soviet people just laughed instead of working harder. On the other hand, a baseball team that sees itself as a legitimate contender for the World Series is likely to be inspired by that vision and to make prodigious efforts to achieve it.

How can you be sure that your vision is realistic, yet challenging? You can never be 100 percent certain, but you can solicit feedback on the vision from those most responsible for making it happen. You can also test the vision with knowledgeable outsiders in a position to judge how other organizations may respond to your initiatives. In the end, however, as long as the vision appears attainable — even if it requires extraordinary efforts and some lucky breaks for it to be achieved — don't be afraid to stretch a little and go for it.

**3.    Reduce the possibility of unpleasant surprises.** There are three sources of surprise: something you expect to happen doesn't, something you don't expect to happen does, and something you never even thought about happens, with unfortunate consequences for your vision. Obviously, by definition, there will always be surprises, but the domain of surprise can be reduced and the negative effects of surprises can be ameliorated.

There are several ways to reduce surprises or to lessen their impact. One is to be quite thorough in forecasting and anticipating the full range of possible future events, drawing on the best experts available, refusing to be lulled into conventional wisdom, and thinking of the future always in terms of alternative scenarios. Another is to build flexibility into the vision statement itself, not getting too specific where it is not necessary to do so. A third approach is to track trends and developments carefully after implementation, as we have discussed in this chapter, to gain the greatest amount of lead time possible to prevent or react to them. And finally, you can build a flexible response capability into the organization so that surprises can be absorbed without too much trauma.

**4.    Watch out for organizational inertia.** It is natural for organizations to resist change, and this chapter showed how it is possible to overcome some kinds of resistance. Remember, however, that you should never be overly constrained by the existing organization. While the culture of the organization tends to endure, alterations are possible. New people can be added who are favorable to the vision, just as AT&T hired people from IBM and other computer companies when it shifted from a protected monopoly to an aggressive competitor. And sometimes a reorganization is all that is needed to break organizational inertia and establish new patterns of relationships.

5. *Don't be too preoccupied with the bottom line.* A vision statement should not focus on the bottom line because doing so makes it much more difficult for people to think long term and strategically. If you concentrate on doing the right thing, the bottom line almost certainly will improve — perhaps even surprisingly so — in the long run. When it comes to making hard choices, many progressive companies rate their customers first in priority, their workers second, and investors only third. They know that if they do the right thing, they will secure the loyalty and support of customers and workers, and rewards to investors will follow; but if they worry first about the bottom line, they are likely to make decisions that cut corners in the marketplace or fail to engage the workers, and in the long run, the investors will suffer the most.

6. *Be flexible and patient in implementing the vision.* Once the proper sense of direction has been determined and people in the organization have bought into the idea, there are always many different ways of getting there. By delegating implementation decisions to those closest to the issues at hand and by allowing employees considerable flexibility in how they choose to implement the vision, you are allowing others to take ownership of the vision and experience pride in achieving it. Apart from the energizing aspects of such an approach, it allows for many small experiments and learning experiences to take place and also insulates the organization from major errors that almost surely would follow from top-down planning or supervision.

7. *Never get complacent.* Just because your vision may be working well at this moment, don't assume it will last forever.

Remember that the easiest time to begin a change in direction is when things are going well for your organization, because then the confidence and resources are amply available. On the other hand, the worst thing to do is let the situation deteriorate to the point where only crisis measures can avoid total failure, because then nobody wants to hear about a new dream. The best time to turn around a battleship is at the first sign of danger, not after the torpedoes have started to land.

To conclude, your job as a visionary leader is to set the direction and personally commit to it, to spread visionary leadership throughout your organization, to empower employees to act, to listen and watch for feedback, and to always focus your attention on helping the organization achieve its greatest potential. Leaders are immortalized for their vision and for their organization's achievements. When your tenure is over and you pass the mantle on to someone else, you want that person to be able to say, "There was a person who helped us see how great we could be, and who laid the foundations for our great leap forward."

# CHAPTER 9

# Developing Visionary Leadership: Securing the Future

Let the word go forth from this time and place,
to friend and foe alike, that the torch has
been passed to a new generation of
Americans.
—JOHN F. KENNEDY

If you want to understand the future of visionary leadership, you need to follow the still unfolding tale of Bill Gates. The energetic founder of the Microsoft Corporation has built a personal fortune of some $5 billion by the tender age of thirty-five almost entirely on the basis of outstanding visionary leadership. The *New York Times* captured his secret quite perceptively: "As a youth, Bill Gates envisioned the future and became a billionaire. Now, as Chairman of Microsoft, he still claims to see what his competitors don't" (Moody, 1991, p. 26).

Bill Gates, like many of his high school classmates, was considered a computer nerd. Unlike the others, however, he took the initiative to start his first two companies at the age of fourteen—one to produce a class scheduling program and the other a traffic counting system. The companies lasted only a short time, but five years later he dropped out of Harvard to write a mainframe computer language for the Altair 8800, a microcomputer kit designed for hobbyists and sold through *Popular Electronics* magazine. From that small beginning came the seeds of Microsoft Corporation, a fast-growing software colossus with over 8,000 employees that dominates its industry, far outranking in size, influence, and capability any of its more than 14,000 competitors.

Bill Gates didn't get an M.B.A. from Stanford; indeed he holds no college degree at all. Nor did he become a remarkable leader by patiently working his way up a chain of management promotions. He is smart, experimental, and persistent, but probably no more so than thousands of his colleagues. And while many people admire his accomplishments, no one has ever accused him of being charismatic, and some don't even think he's a very nice guy.

But all this doesn't matter. The secret of Bill Gates's extraordinary success can be stated in one simple phrase: *he built Microsoft from the start as a twenty-first–century organization, and he runs it with a highly developed sense of visionary leadership.* The story of Bill Gates is a window on the future of visionary leadership. To understand why this is so, we must examine the forces that are shaping today's leading-edge organizations and their implications for the future of visionary leadership.

# TWENTY-FIRST–CENTURY ORGANIZATIONS

Modern organizations are being buffeted and shaped by many powerful forces in their external environments, a few of which are listed in Table 9.1. As a result of these and other forces, the outlines of the new twenty-first–century organizations are becoming clear. Some of their characteristics are listed below:

■ *The labor force consists primarily of highly skilled knowledge workers.* At Microsoft, these workers comprise nearly the entire labor force, since anyone who is not a programmer, system designer, or word processor is likely to be a manager,

Table 9.1. Some Forces Shaping
Twenty-First–Century Organizations.

1. Explosive technological change caused by simultaneous and mutually reinforcing breakthroughs in materials, genetics, information sciences, space technology, automation, and instrumentation
2. The dominance of postindustrial economies based on information, knowledge, education, and services
3. The globalization of business, politics, culture, and environmental concerns
4. The restructuring of national economies to accommodate intense international competition, and the gradual transition from military to economic dominance in global affairs
5. The erosion of confidence in all institutions, including governments, families, and religion, and the resultant search for self-sufficiency and meaning in work and grass roots activism
6. High economic stress resulting from heavy debt loads, global competition, vulnerable banking systems, and deferred costs of a decaying infrastructure and environmental cleanup
7. Demographic and sociocultural shifts toward far more diversity and fragmentation of values, life-styles, and tastes
8. Relative affluence in material goods coupled with "new" scarcities (for example, job security and parental time for children) and increased personal risks from crime and environmental pollution

accountant, salesperson, lawyer, or service worker. Knowledge workers are quite different from production workers in that they tend to view themselves as professionals and they operate on their own initiative. They also consider psychic rewards like challenge, status, personal growth, and self-esteem as important as their paychecks. In an organization with such a labor force, hiring, motivating, training, and retaining workers becomes a major determinant of long-term success. Also, networks often replace hierarchies in such organizations to facilitate communications and coordination among knowledge workers.

■ *The products or services consist primarily of packages of knowledge.* This is obvious at a firm like Microsoft, where all the products are software and accompanying operating manuals, or in a movie company, where only a tiny fraction of the total value produced is represented by the film itself. It is less obvious, but equally true, at pharmaceutical companies, banks, government agencies, and most service firms. In fact, the production of most products for which the knowledge component is small, such as shoes or small appliances, has long since left the developed countries for the third world to take advantage of the lower cost of unskilled labor. What production is left is of products and services with small amounts of materials and large doses of human intelligence and skill.

■ *They tend to be global in scope.* If their customers or clients are not distributed globally—Microsoft generates more sales and profits overseas than at home—then their competitors often are. At the very least, they are likely to need supplies, technologies, ideas, or equipment from overseas. Most organizations already have a multicultural work force reflecting a variety of ethnic and national origins. Even a purely local organization is no longer totally immune from the impact of distant events that affect local interest rates, government policies, or the attitudes and expectations of workers or customers.

■ *They tend to be technologically driven or, at least, highly technologically sensitive.* This is obvious at Microsoft, which is very much driven by rapid developments in the performance characteristics of personal computers as well as new concepts of software design and use. However, it is just as true of banks, universities, or the Internal Revenue Service, not to mention food processors, automobile manufacturers, or military organizations. Thus, the management of transitions from one generation of product or process technologies to another, a skill that Bill Gates has mastered, has become a major challenge and potential cost trap for twenty-first–century organizations.

■ *They tend to be characterized by rapid change and complexity.* Microsoft, for example, is caught in a positive feedback loop in which advances in hardware stimulate the demand for new software, which in turn, creates new demand for even more powerful computers, and so on. As a result, the pace of change is so swift that even before a new piece of software is introduced into the market, work has begun on developing its successor. Research is constantly aimed at producing new ideas that will make current concepts obsolete. Innovation in products and processes has become the engine that drives the economic system. As a result, however large the organization, it must retain the agility to react quickly and appropriately to myriad threats and opportunities.

■   *Their activities are distributed over space and time.* In a company like Microsoft, system designers work at odd hours, and many of them telecommute from home, at least part of the time. Work goes on not just around the clock but around the globe, as transactions and interactions take place in "info-space" and are transmitted instantly and simultaneously to all who need to know. Because knowledge workers are often dispersed in time and space and because they view themselves as professionals expected to exercise initiative, these organizations tend to be flatter, less hierarchical, and more intricately networked than is common today. To function at all in such an environment, organizations must cultivate a high level of mutual trust, which in turn, implies an organizational need for high ethical standards and integrity.

■   *They tend to be multipurpose, serving the needs of many constituencies.* Microsoft, for example, is driven first and foremost by its need to provide high-quality, innovative products for its customers. However, it also caters to the needs of its highly talented work force, for whom it provides everything from educational opportunities and pregnancy leaves to athletic facilities and social events. Beyond that, Microsoft must satisfy the profit expectations of Wall Street, be a responsible community member at every plant location, contribute to the knowledge base in its field, and be a good corporate citizen. Thus, twenty-first–century organizations are never simply economic institutions or social institutions or political, artistic, environmental, or any other single form of institution; they are rather a melding of all or several of these types in different proportions.

■   *They tend to have fuzzy boundaries.* No leading-edge organization, no matter how large, is able to do everything it needs to do to achieve its vision on its own. Even corporations as large as AT&T and IBM are constantly searching for joint venture partners or collaborators. Often boundaries are extended right into the offices of a supplier, as in so-called just-in-time production, or into the home of a customer, as with on-line shopping. At Microsoft, relationships with hardware manufacturers are so close and the firms' destinies so intertwined with joint-design efforts and technology sharing, that institutional boundaries are necessarily blurred and permeable. As a result, Microsoft is privy to most of the secrets of the industry and benefits from technical expertise far beyond its own.

These eight characteristics of twenty-first–century organizations—using knowledge workers to produce knowledge-based products and services, being driven by technological innovation and rapid change, having a global scope, with operations distributed over time and space, and serving multiple constituencies with many collaborative arrangements—suggest both challenges and opportunities for visionary leaders.

# IMPLICATIONS FOR
# VISIONARY LEADERS

If someone like Bill Gates thrives in the type of organization just described, it is because he is an outstanding visionary leader. Consider the following observation about him:

Among the things that set Gates apart from those who started out with him is an ability to foresee the practical utility of distant technology. When studying future advances in computing, he always asks himself, "What will that create a demand for?" In 1975—six years before the first IBM personal computer hit the market—Gates and Allen wrote out a vision to inspire themselves: "A personal computer on every desk and in every home." Today, while the rest of the world is still coming to grips with that 16-year-old vision, Gates has already invested six years and hundreds of millions of dollars in multimedia computing which integrates sound, moving pictures, still pictures and text—all in the personal computer [Moody, 1991, p. 28].

In other words, Gates is not just thinking about how to compete with other software companies or even how to carve out a piece of IBM or Apple. He is way beyond that, thinking ahead to the day when his primary competitors will be the Japanese consumer electronic firms who have sold hundreds of millions of television sets, VCRs, and compact disk players. He is not merely forecasting a convergence of personal computer technologies with entertainment media—he fully intends to make it happen! Bill Gates understands that only by taking the initiative, by dreaming the dream and putting his full resources and commitment behind it, will he be able to point the way for Microsoft in an industry that is increasingly chaotic, fragmented, and dispersed.

We need to develop this theme a bit further. What are the full ramifications of twenty-first–century organizations for the future of visionary leadership?

First, and most obvious, the twenty-first–century organization virtually demands visionary leadership. It cannot function without it, for an organization driven by accelerating technological change, staffed by a diverse, multicultural mix of highly intelligent knowledge workers, facing global complexity, a vast kaleidoscope of individual customer needs, and the incessant demands of multiple constituencies would simply self-destruct without a common sense of direction. Conflicting forces and agendas would explode the organization into thousands of bits of human shrapnel speeding off in every direction, only rarely hitting a meaningful target.

In such an organization, visionary leadership is vital not only to provide a force field to align thousands of disparate tasks but because there is no way to tap the energies or genius of knowledge workers without it. The more highly skilled and professional the workers, the more critical it becomes for the leader to be able to supply a meaningful job context and a challenge worthy of commitment and exceptional effort. Skilled professionals do not want to waste their time, and they don't have to because they can easily move to where the action is and where they can make a difference — that is, to organizations that know where they are going and why it is important to get there. That's why power in twenty-first–century organizations tends to flow to those who have the capacity to challenge and inspire highly skilled professionals.

The powerful attraction of visionary leadership for knowledge workers is abundantly in evidence at Microsoft, where programmers routinely work long hours on their own time to complete projects and claim they're having fun doing it. Microsoft does not offer higher salaries and bonuses or more perks than many of its peers. Yet its turnover is very low, and it is able to hire only the most outstanding professionals in its field, less than 1 percent of all who apply for jobs!

While becoming more important in all organizations, the visioning process is likely to occur more frequently in twenty-first–century organizations. The rate of change and the effects of global complexity conspire to make any particular vision useful for only a limited time. As the quote about Bill Gates suggests, visionary leaders will have to be a step ahead of competitors, dreaming about what the future holds and what role the organization should play in it. Visionary leadership will be as indispensable for renewing existing organizations as for starting up new entrepreneurial ventures.

At the same time, visionary leadership, while crucial at

the top, is also becoming necessary at lower levels in the organization. The need for agility in responding to changes in markets and technology and the geographical dispersion of operations around the globe make it impossible to sustain centralized decision making. This creates a demand for millions of visionary leaders at the lower levels of organizations, leaders who are able to establish a sense of direction for their own units that supports the overall organizational vision and yet enables those units to position themselves in anticipation of changes in their local circumstances. For example, many twenty-first–century corporations like Microsoft have a great number of "intrapreneurs," visionary leaders inside the organization charged with creating new product or market thrusts that will become the mainstream of tomorrow's operations. The same concept applies equally well at organizations as diverse as United Way, a university, a large hospital, or a social action group such as Mothers Against Drunk Driving.

The twenty-first–century organization also accentuates the role of the visionary leader as change agent, promoting experimentation, creating a sense of urgency for change, and establishing corporate cultures in which risk taking and broad participation are highly valued. Bill Gates, for example, who enjoys nothing so much as brainstorming new product ideas with his technical staff, has made it a cornerstone of his leadership style to spread himself around and make himself available to everyone in the organization, if not actually in person, then by electronic mail. He does all he can to make Microsoft, despite its current giant size, continue to feel like the small, personal, nimble company it once was.

This balance between vision and action, which has the power to literally create the future, was expressed with great beauty and insight by Henry Wadsworth Longfellow in a poem called "Keramos":

Thine was the prophet's vision, thine
The exaltation, the divine
Insanity of noble minds,

That never falters nor abates,
But labors and endures and waits,
Till all that it foresees it finds,
Or what it cannot find creates!

Finally, all this serves to accentuate the need to select and develop new visionary leaders with great care and to plan deliberately for leadership transitions. The need for effective visionary leadership is becoming so great as to pose a critical challenge to all concerned with education, including parents, schools, universities, and in-house training programs.

# EDUCATION FOR VISIONARY LEADERS

Look at the life story of a visionary leader and it is unlikely you will find much in the way of specific training for leadership. Thus far, most people who have succeeded as visionary leaders seem to have been self-selected and self-made. Bill Gates received no leadership education, nor did Ted Turner, Wayne Huizenga, Frances Hesselbein, Steve Jobs, Walt Disney, or any of the others mentioned in this book. And apart from an active curiosity, some basic intelligence, and the ability to learn from experience, they seem to have had no remarkable genetic endowment predisposing them to leadership success. They are people who figured out for themselves how to dream dreams, enthuse others with their visions, and then make them happen.

From a societal viewpoint, however, this is a reckless hit-and-miss process. If millions of new visionary leaders are needed in twenty-first–century organizations, then leaving their development to the random processes of self-selection and self-development in a society awash with other temptations and distractions for young people certainly will lead to serious gaps in leadership, as already seems to be the case. Isn't there a better way? If we got serious about producing a larger number of effective visionary leaders, what could be done? More specifically, what can you, who are already a leader, do to help others become more effective leaders?

If you are a parent, there is much you can do to help your youngsters prepare for future roles as visionary leaders. To start, make sure your children develop early a sense of self-esteem. People who have little self-respect lack the confidence to pursue their own best ideas and find it difficult to earn the respect of others. Encourage your children to be experimental, to try many things, and to assume responsibility. Praise them lavishly for any accomplishments. Your respect and admiration for your children's growing skills and competencies provide the foundation on which their self-esteem will be built.

Stimulate your children's imagination and creativity, for these will be the source of their visions and dreams when they become leaders. Fantasize with them, praise their drawings, encourage them to read science fiction, make up mind games to play with them, and never miss an opportunity to show your appreciation for a fanciful or clever observation.

Develop your children's communications skills, both oral and written. Without exception, visionary leaders are able to communicate their visions to others so they are thoroughly understood and accepted. Encourage your children to act in plays, keep diaries, write letters, and actively participate in table talk. Most of all, be a good listener when they get excited about something and share their enthusiasm for their ideas.

Place the highest priority on helping your children learn how to learn. Visionary leaders are virtual learning machines, skilled at accumulating ideas and knowledge from a great variety of sources and putting them together in novel ways to discern new patterns and directions. Show your children that learning is fun. Be a role model of lifelong learning. Give them a variety of new experiences and challenge them to create games or write stories about them.

Find out what your children enjoy and most naturally

take to. Encourage them in those areas. In a world where work and play are progressively harder to separate, it is better to enjoy both than neither, and one of the marks of a visionary leader is the ability to harness playful and creative attitudes in a work setting.

Finally, teach them about the leaders you admire or the great leaders of history, whether they're in religion, politics, sports, or whatever. Visionary leaders are people who know that individuals can make a big difference. Your children should appreciate early in life that they too can make a difference. Maybe they won't start a company at age fourteen like Bill Gates, but they can make things happen at their school or on a sports team or in the neighborhood. Encourage them to take responsibility for the problems they see all around them.

Educational institutions at every level, from kindergartens to universities, also need to play a responsible role in the creation of future visionary leaders. If you have some influence at your local school or college, help them rethink their academic agendas. Schools now spend most of their time conveying knowledge, socializing students into the norms of the larger society, and developing critical, analytical, and communications skills. All of these are important to visionary leaders, but a vital missing link is problem-finding, as opposed to problem-solving, skills. It is no longer enough for students to master the received knowledge and wisdom of their elders. If they are to be visionary leaders, they need to be able to break with the past and synthesize new directions. Instead of conducting experiments or analyzing problems with known solutions, students need to learn how to design their own experiments and how to conceptualize and address new problems.

Schools are obsessed with the past. Undoubtedly, students need to know how and why their current society and its institutions evolved, but if they are to be visionary leaders, they also need to learn how to think about the future in a systematic fashion. For every history book they are asked to read, they should be challenged to write a scenario of the future in such key areas as economics, ecology, international relations, and social values.

Every school should encourage students (and perhaps even require them) to have leadership experiences while still in school. Such experience may involve being a team captain, heading a campus club, starting a special interest group, or leading any of the hundreds of activities that go on all the time in schools, from plays and newspapers to proms and fundraisers.

Schools should include leadership itself as an important subject for study. Students could study the lives of great leaders like Lincoln and Churchill; analyze major leadership decisions that led to events like the invasion of the Bay of Pigs, the New Deal, or the march on Washington; interview local leaders or invite them to campus for detailed discussions about the challenges and opportunities they face; or conduct conferences around vision statements for critical current issues in their communities. They could also learn about the history and philosophy of leadership, leadership strategies, and leadership ethics.

And, of course, schools should teach how organizations work. Since most of modern work—and all of leadership—takes place in organizations, it is important for future leaders to understand organizational cultures, structures, and processes: how organizations are started, how they grow, and why they decline; how decisions are made; and how information technologies are employed. Students also need to acquire organizational skills such as teamwork, negotiation, entrepreneurship, and networking and to learn how to cooperate in multicultural settings.

Finally, there is much you can do inside your own organization to stimulate the development of visionary leaders. You can start by making the organization as decentralized, flat, and flexible as possible, giving people on the lower levels lots of responsibility and considerable discretion for what happens in their units. This alone will create dozens of potential leadership roles. Demand that the heads of these units develop visions and strategies and reward them for their initiative and courage at least as much as you recognize their shorter-term accomplishments.

Hire people for their leadership potential. Perhaps the best indicator of such potential is a track record of successful leadership somewhere else. Since not all potential leaders have had the opportunity to prove themselves at prior jobs, look for evidence of visionary leadership throughout their life experiences, possibly at college, in a church group, on a community council, in a political action group, or on a Little League team. The context is less important than evidence that the individual is willing to accept responsibility, exercise initiative, and develop a meaningful sense of direction for himself or herself and others to follow.

Having once hired some potential visionary leaders, give them a variety of experiences that will allow them to exercise their skills, develop a perspective on the organization, and establish the communications networks they will need as they move up the organization. Have them operate in different divisions, perform different functions, or work in different cultures. Put them on task forces, ask them to start up new operations, or challenge them to turn around an ineffective unit.

Don't neglect their formal education either. Expose them to outside experts and ideas. Encourage them to learn all they can about the organization's current and evolving technologies. Conduct meetings to explore future developments and ask them to read books on leadership that you find particularly useful.

Last, and by no means least, serve as a mentor to these future leaders, for they are the best hope for the long-term viability of your organization. Be a role model. Discuss your concerns with them. Seek their advice on new visions you may be considering. Treat them as colleagues in the constant search for organizational renewal. Help them learn and grow and show your appreciation for their contributions to your organization's success.

# TAKING CHARGE

Perhaps the best way to end this book is by revisiting the opening sentence:

> There is no more powerful engine driving an organization toward excellence and long-range success than an attractive, worthwhile, and achievable vision of the future, widely shared.

You now know how to develop such a vision and why it is so vital for your organization. It remains only to point out that there are millions of people out there — workers, young people, and ordinary citizens — starved for a sense of direction. As an example, consider the following letter to Ann Landers that appeared in hundreds of newspapers nationwide on March 23, 1989:

Dear Ann Landers:

I am a 23 year old college graduate (business major). I don't presume to speak for my generation, but I know what I feel.

People wonder about us. They say we are materialistic, just out for ourselves. They say we are apathetic. It must go deeper than that. Teens are committing suicide in record numbers. What is wrong with us? Just look around.

The media reach far and wide, bringing stories from all over the world. We have overpopulation, the environment is being destroyed, our natural resources are dwindling. People are oppressed, starving and killing each other. There are enough weapons to blow up the world we live in 40 times! AIDS continues to spread and there is no vaccine and no cure.

On the home front, the United States is faltering. The national debt is at an incomprehensible level. Homeless people freeze to death on the streets. Gang violence, alcoholism and drug abuse are rampant. Teens are having babies out of wedlock and many will never get off welfare.

Not many people my age will be able to own a house, no matter what their educational level or whom they work for. Takeovers and mergers ruin the hopes of job security. Many of us expect to have a lower standard of living than our parents. The U.S. is losing its edge in the world market.

It sounds hopeless. But I love this country, and I think there is hope. I don't believe my generation is apathetic. *We just don't know where to start.*

> **Waiting for Guidance in California**

Multiply this one voice by millions and it adds up to a stirring call to action. A desperate sense of dissatisfaction with the present and a muffled cry for hope for a better future—what else can it be but the beginning of a grass roots search for vision? It is not a thousand—or even a million—points of light that are needed but hundreds of powerful beacons to show the way.

Bill Gates is one of those beacons. Will you be the next?

# Visionary Leadership for the Public Sector

The popular image of a government agency is that of a large bureaucratic machine endlessly processing papers, making decisions, and providing services mandated by courts or legislative bodies. Behind the popular image, however, are a large number of individual civil servants, many of them highly educated and possessing considerable professional pride, working together in agencies, departments, bureaus, and local offices doing their best to provide important public services. Since they have as great a need for leadership as workers in other organizations, they too need a vision to guide them, for the same reasons discussed earlier.

Of course, the contexts and operating styles of a public agency are much different from those in the private sector. The environment is more complex too, with legislative and executive bodies at all levels constantly issuing directives, the courts endlessly interpreting and reinterpreting legal obligations and boundaries, the media and special interest groups monitoring and reacting to every initiative, and budgets under unremitting pressure. Still, there is plenty of scope for visionary leadership in the public sector. All government executives hope to move their departments or agencies in a socially useful direction—or at least should aspire to do so—and to leave their mark not just as competent administrators but as responsible visionary leaders.

This Appendix illustrates the same systematic approach to developing a new vision—here applied to a public sector organization—that we used in Part Two with the Prime Pet Foods example. The concepts—and questions—are the same. To demonstrate how this approach works in a public sector organization, consider a Department of Parks and Recreation in a medium-sized state. Assume that a new director, just appointed, is seeking to energize the department with a challenging new vision to guide its activities over the next five years. To begin, let's see how she might answer the questions posed in Chapter Three.

# THE VISION AUDIT

*1. What is the current stated mission or purpose of your organization?*

The director finds the current mission well defined in the legislation establishing the department. Although far too lengthy to quote here, the essence of the mission is to work with other agencies, both public and private, to provide recreational opportunities and programs for all citizens and visitors to the state, to operate and maintain the state park system, and to administer state and federal funds allocated to these purposes. Many of the tasks of the department are of a coordinative nature, working with such federal agencies as the U.S. Forest Service, the Army Corps of Engineers, and the Bureau of Land Management; state agencies such as the Departments of Transportation, Tourism, and Education; county and local recreation departments; and a vast array of private recreation-

oriented groups such as YMCAs, sports clubs, and environmental organizations.

### 2. *What value does the organization provide to society?*

The Department of Parks and Recreation provides citizens and visitors with access to a broad range of recreational
opportunities such as hiking, fishing, water sports, hunting,
and so forth. Recreation has long been recognized as a basic
societal need, enriching individual lives, providing experiences that allow human beings to develop their skills and
talents, and contributing to people's physical and emotional
well-being.

### 3. *What is the character of the industry or institutional framework within which your organization operates?*

Recreational services and facilities are provided by many
organizations. The public sector owns or has jurisdiction over
the recreational use of public lands, forests, rivers and lakes,
beaches, and the like. A strong nonprofit sector offers recreational opportunities through hiking clubs, YMCAs, various
scouting and Outward Bound groups, and amateur sports
leagues. So does a vigorously competitive private sector that
includes golf courses, camp grounds, equipment suppliers,
professional spectator sports, summer camps, and fitness centers. Each sector operates with considerable autonomy and
owes its allegiance to particular user groups. The State Department of Parks and Recreation has the broadest mandate and is
responsible to all citizens. It also is responsible for coordinating
its activities with myriad other federal, state, and local agencies
concerned with water, energy, the environment, criminal justice, and regional planning.

### 4. *What is your organization's unique position in that industry or institutional structure?*

The Department of Parks and Recreation is a cabinet-
level department reporting to the governor of the state. It is

charged with providing leadership to other agencies in managing lands, facilities, and services to meet the recreational needs of the entire state population. Its budget and legislative agenda are provided by elected officials in the state legislature; its expenditures and activities are monitored by other state agencies, committees of the legislature, and various activist groups. The policies and decisions of the department, which are often controversial, are widely publicized and criticized in the press and elsewhere, and conflicts between the department and other interested parties sometimes wind up in the court system.

### 5. What does it take for your organization to succeed?

To be successful, the department must use its resources efficiently and wisely, avoiding any taint of scandal. It must also be fair to all its constituencies, maintain good relations with the governor's office and legislative committees, and be responsive to public interest advocates and the media. Other critical success factors include the quality of state-operated services; the extent to which the department can coordinate and marshal the resources of other agencies, public and private; and the degree of public satisfaction with the recreational opportunities made available.

### 6. What are the values and the organizational culture that govern behavior and decision making?

The values of the department include a strong dedication to public service, ethical management of state resources, and careful adherence to legal and legislative guidelines. Many of the workers in the department consider themselves professionals and take pride in upholding the standards of their professions. Successful innovation, while recognized and celebrated, is relatively rare because most workers consider the rewards insufficient to outweigh the very heavy risks of exposing the department or the governor to criticism or legal action if an innovation were to go wrong. Education and training are highly valued and recognized as essential for promotion. Information is a much-prized commodity, and considerable time is spent networking to keep informed about the latest rumors on budget cuts, rule changes, and personnel transfers.

The organizational culture puts a premium on teamwork, as most important decisions are made in committee meetings, which take up much of the time of managers in the department. Most other decisions and authorizations are handled hierarchically in the classic bureaucratic tradition. Communications, memoranda, and formal documentation are considered important because of legal requirements but are sometimes taken to excess to protect individuals and units from exposure to criticism. Since firing is strictly regulated by civil service rules, poor performers are rarely punished, although those so designated may be ostracized or shifted to undesirable locations.

### 7. *What are the operating strengths and weaknesses of the organization?*

Please see Table A.1.

Table A.1. Strengths and Weaknesses of the
Department of Parks and Recreation.

| Strengths | Weaknesses |
| --- | --- |
| 1. Excellent state parks and facilities | 1. Poor maintenance of roads leading to and in the parks |
| 2. Increasing demand for recreational services | 2. Insufficient staff to handle growing tourist load |
| 3. Supportive lobby and constituency | 3. Severe budget cuts in last several years |
| 4. Generally scandal free | 4. Several major lawsuits pending |
| 5. Good relations with legislature | 5. Strained relations with current governor's staff |
| 6. Well-respected director | 6. Under pressure from environmentalists to protect wilderness from overuse |
| 7. Experienced core professional staff | 7. Unable to meet special recreational needs |
| 8. Good training programs | 8. Hyperactive rumor mill |

8. *What is the current strategy, and can it be defended?*

The department tries to comply with all its legislative mandates as best it can with limited staff and a declining budget. Emphasis is on efficiency and cost reduction. In cases of conflict over resources, the department gives priority to core service programs in the state parks, to programs that can be funded by the federal government, and to highly visible environmental protection projects. Capital projects are being deferred, despite overcrowding of existing facilities and a growing demand for services.

The current strategy will be difficult to sustain over the long term. Parks and facilities are not being adequately maintained, while demands for their use are increasing. After several years of cost cutting, additional increments of efficiency will be much harder to obtain.

9. *Does the organization have a clearly stated vision? If so, what is it?*

The Department of Parks and Recreation does not have its own clearly stated vision beyond the intentions reflected in its legislative mandates, which tend to be broad, somewhat unrealistic, and often contradictory statements like "providing a full range of high-quality recreational opportunities to all residents in the state, regardless of race, color, gender, or physical handicap, while ensuring the protection of all species in state park lands."

10. *If the organization continues on its current path, where will it be heading over the next decade? How good would such a direction be?*

If the department continues over the next decade on the path of the last five years, its staff will be cut by at least 50 percent and most of the state parks will have to close for all but a few months a year. Services will be so scarce that reservations for park use will have to be made months — perhaps years — in advance. Tourism into the state will be adversely affected, and nearly all recreation will be offered on a fee-for-service basis, making it essentially unavailable to lower-income citizens. The department will not be able to maintain the parks at a reasonable level or protect the species in them. The department's effectiveness will be so severely impaired that it will be merged with another state department to share personnel.

Such an outcome is not likely to be acceptable to the public, the tourism industry, environmentalists, or health authorities. Another vision is sorely needed.

*11. Do the key people in the organization know where the organization is headed and agree on the direction?*

Every manager in the department understands the irreconcilability of increased demands for services with budget cuts; they all agree that the department's ability to serve is declining rapidly. In the absence of a more encouraging vision, morale is at a low point, and some have already taken early retirement or left for jobs in the private sector. Many others fear for their jobs.

*12. Do the structures, processes, personnel, incentives, and information systems support the current direction of the organization?*

No. The department remains organized and staffed as it was in an earlier time of more ample budgets. If the image of decline is correct, the department will have to be reorganized to consolidate staffs, more efficient procedures will be needed, and incentives will have to be tied to cost cutting rather than service provision. A revised vision of the future role of the department is needed to guide this consolidation.

# THE VISION SCOPE

By its very nature, a public sector organization is responsive to a much wider array of influences and interests than that of the average corporation, making the task of scoping the vision for such an agency much more complicated. However, this is a challenge that must be met if the agency is to have any hope of rising above special interests and short-term political pressures and moving in a coherent long-term direction to serve the public interest.

In the last section, our vision audit revealed the State Department of Parks and Recreation to be an agency with multiple missions, operating in a complex environment amid continual pressures to cut costs and improve services. Some redirection and refocusing of the department's efforts seem essential. Now we ask what the scope of the new direction should be, by answering the very same questions posed to Prime Pet Foods in Chapter Four.

*1.  Who are the most critical stakeholders — both inside and outside your organization — and of these, which are the most important?*
The key stakeholders for the department are:

- Users of recreational facilities and services, a diverse population that can be further classified into various demographic categories such as age, income, ethnicity, and so on

- Governmental providers of recreational services or facilities, such as federal agencies (Department of the Interior, National Park Service), other state agencies, and regional and local jurisdictions

- Nongovernmental providers of recreational services, which include private and nonprofit organizations, the tourist industry, and other organizations

- Suppliers of equipment and services

- Regulators and legislators at the federal, state, and local levels

- Special interest groups such as environmentalists and

advocacy organizations (for example, for the disabled, for hunting and fishing interests)

- The media, especially publications devoted to sports and leisure pursuits

- Educators

- Private landowners

- The real estate and community development industry

- Medical, health care, and insurance industries

- Organized sports, arts, entertainment, and other industries that offer alternatives to public parks and recreational activities

- Taxpayers

All of these stakeholders are important to the department and constrain its activities. However, the most important ones are probably the various user communities, governmental and nongovernmental providers of recreational services, special interest groups, and taxpayers.

**2. *What are the major interests and expectations of the five or six most important stakeholders regarding the future of your organization?***
The interests and expectations of the major stakeholders include the following:

User Communities

- Wide diversity of recreational opportunities

- Easy access

- Economical to use

- Locational convenience

- Fair and equitable allocation of resources

- Safety and security
- High-quality experience
- Well-maintained facilities

Governmental Providers of Recreational Services

- Obtain sufficient tax support
- Provide services not available from the private sector
- Conserve resources for future generations
- Avoid controversy
- Preserve the bureaucracy
- Promote efficiency and productivity
- Provide equitable resource allocation
- Gain favorable media exposure

Nongovernmental Providers of Recreational Services

- Supplement government services and cultural values
- Provide profits (private sector) or meaningful voluntary experiences (nonprofits)
- Promote enjoyable, significant work settings
- Minimize unnecessary governmental interference
- Encourage efficiency and productivity

Special Interest Groups

- Opportunities for constituents
- Enhancement of public services
- Recognition, image
- Protection of rights

- Favorable legislation and/or administrative decisions

- Participation in decision making

Taxpayers

- Efficiency and productivity of governmental services

- Fairness and equity in resource distribution

- Quality and value in facilities and recreational opportunities provided

- Honesty and integrity of public sector employees

- Environmental responsibility — departmental stewardship of parks and natural resources for future generations

### 3.   *What threats or opportunities emanate from these critical stakeholders?*

Those who use state park and recreational services offer several opportunities, of which the most important from the department's viewpoint is the possibility that users may be willing to pay considerably more for the use of facilities and services, especially those that can be tailored to their use. For example, campers may be willing to pay extra for cleanup services, wilderness guides, cellular telephone rental, or secure parking. The department may also be able to find additional financial support from federal government and charitable grants for special recreational services for targeted populations such as the disabled, the elderly, inner-city children, and so forth. Apart from money, user populations may form support and advocacy groups for certain kinds of services, thereby exercising influence with legislatures and the governor's office.

On the other hand, user groups may pose threats, especially if one or more of them is displeased with the levels of service provided or feel that its interests are being neglected. User groups are in a position to lobby for their special needs, such as the removal of architectural barriers for disabled people. They also might support tighter regulatory controls on the department's activities or seek media attention for their grievances, as fishing and hunting interests have done for many years.

Other providers of recreational services, both public and private, offer the opportunity of relieving pressures on state facilities by offering users alternatives that are more convenient or in some ways more attractive. For example, many campers these days are willing to pay extra for the facilities of private campgrounds, and some hunters head for private lands and resorts rather than public property. Some organizations, like the Boy Scouts and the YMCAs, have for years helped to educate the public on the responsible use of wilderness areas. Environmental groups may be instrumental in gathering support for expanding parklands and conserving natural resources.

On the other hand, other providers of recreational services may pose threats. The National Park Service, U.S. Forest Service, Bureau of Land Management, and other federal agencies concerned with such activities as transportation, energy, or agriculture may have agendas that will limit the department's activities. Similarly, other state and local agencies concerned with such matters as housing, health, education, and the environment may oppose or even challenge initiatives that the Parks Department considers within its mandate and vital for its constituencies.

Finally, taxpayers have the ultimate power of the purse and may or may not be willing to support state recreational initiatives at any particular time. One possible consequence might be taxpayer support for mandating private sector contributions to recreational facilities in exchange for development rights.

*4. Considering yourself a stakeholder, what do you personally and passionately want to make happen in your organization?*

The director of the State Department of Parks and Recreation, as the leader of the agency, may have a personal agenda that will affect the vision of the department. For example, the director might have been a legislator well known for fiscal prudence and cost cutting and, in fact, may have been appointed for that quality. In this case, we will assume she has a lifelong commitment to environmental preservation and desires to leave the job with a reputation for responsible stewardship of natural resources.

**5.    What are the boundaries to your new vision? For example, are there time, geographical, or social constraints?**

Because major changes in direction for the department could easily take five to ten years to implement, a new vision should be targeted at least that far out. The geographical scope in this case is determined by the state boundaries. Within those boundaries, the scope must include all types of state-provided parks and recreation facilities and services for all potential users, including ordinary citizens, special interests, and tourists.

**6.    What must the vision accomplish? How will you know when it is successful?**

The success of the new vision can be measured by the extent to which it promotes the following:

Public Satisfaction

- Breadth of participation
- Decrease in frustration, complaint letters

Public Good

- Public health—physical and mental wellness
- Improved quality of life
- Natural resource preservation
- Enhanced tourism

Accessibility of Services and Facilities

- Convenience

- Affordability for users

- Equity—fairness of distribution

Efficiency of Service Delivery

- High value, reasonable cost

- Productivity of state employees and contractors

Service Quality

- Safety

- Adequacy of maintenance

- Enhanced cultural values

Collaboration

- Cooperation with federal agencies

- Cooperation with other state and local agencies

- Cooperation with private and nonprofit sectors

7. *Which critical issues must be addressed in the vision?*
There are certain issues that affect all state recreational agencies and should be addressed in a potential new vision. First, in an era of stable or decreasing taxpayer support for all public services, how will the activities of the department be funded? Second, how can the increasing demand for recreational services (due to population growth, tourism, and growing health consciousness) be reconciled with the need to protect public lands from crowding and environmental damage? Third, how can public and private recreational services be coordinated to enhance the quality, accessibility, and range of recreational opportunities available to citizens in the future?

Finally, how can the recreational experience be enriched so that it is most beneficial for the greatest number of people and offers something for everyone regardless of age, gender, ethnicity, economic status, or disabilities?

Up to this point, we see that the director has determined the need for a new vision for her department and has decided on its scope. It is now time for her—and us—to think about how the future is likely to develop for her organization.

# THE VISION CONTEXT

The State Department of Parks and Recreation is a typical public agency—beset by financing problems, answerable to a wide range of constituents, constrained by many other federal, state, and local agencies, and charged with offering a complex set of services and facilities to myriad users, many with narrow interests, while respecting values such as equity, efficiency, and environmental responsibility. In this section, we carry the analysis into the future by addressing the same questions raised in the Prime Pet Foods example in Chapter Five.

*1. What major changes can be expected in the needs and wants served by your organization in the future?*

   a. More concern for the health and wellness aspects of recreation, as opposed to diversion or amusement

   b. Increased participation in riskier recreation activities, such as rock climbing, white-water rafting, and bungee jumping

   c. Greater need for recreational opportunities close to urban areas

   d. Greater concern for the quality and intensity of recreational experiences, especially those that allow people to develop new skills and grow in their appreciation and understanding of nature

e. More concern for safety and security in the face of increasing use of public lands

f. Greater demand for active recreation by elderly people to preserve vitality and fill time available due to early retirement

g. Increased time available for visiting public recreation facilities because of powerful and highly portable computers and telecommunications equipment, which allow some people to combine recreation with work activities

**2.** *What changes can be expected in the major stakeholders of your organization in the future?*

User Communities

a. Demand for family recreation increases as parents in smaller families and dual-career families seek "quality time" with their children

b. Increased importance of tourism to the state's economy, which makes it necessary to accommodate large numbers of foreign and out-of-state visitors in park facilities

c. Expansion of group tours to parks

d. Increased immigration and heightened sense of ethnic identity create special needs, such as soccer fields, ethnic foods in parks, and multilanguage trail signs

e. Greater recognition of the rights of disabled people to have access to the full range of recreational opportunities

Governmental Providers of Recreational Services

f.  Tighter budgets in all agencies

g.  New federal/state/regional partnerships in land protection

h.  More state influence on management of federal lands

i.  More emphasis on environmental programs

j.  Increased federal and state spending on infrastructure near urban areas

k.  Increasing conflict of water, timber, mining, and oil-drilling interests with environmental considerations, which shapes and limits recreational uses of public lands

Nongovernmental Providers of Recreational Services

l.  Privatization of some public recreational services

m. Increase in theme parks and other man-made destination resorts

n.  Expansion of scouting programs to occupy after-school time of kids of working parents

o.  Increase in employer-sponsored recreational programs

p.  Expansion of leisure-oriented activities of community colleges

Taxpayers

q.  Tax revolts, which prevent tax increases from keeping up with the expanding demand for parks and recreational services

r.  Reduced taxpayer priority for expenditures on recreational services in the face of increased need for funds for education, criminal justice, and economic development

### 3. *What major changes can be expected in the relevant economic environments in the future?*

a. Major recession, perhaps depression, in the state as companies attempt to slim down to meet foreign competition

b. Reduction in real wealth as real estate and stock market prices fall to compensate for excesses of the 1980s

c. Job sharing and thirty-hour workweeks provide more time off, which is used by many workers to moonlight

d. Widening gap between the haves and the have-nots in society and decreased acceptance of welfare

e. Increase in small businesses and entrepreneurship

f. Smaller proportion of working population to overall population

g. Major cost containment program in medical costs

h. Dispersal of work places due to telecommuting and urban problems (for example, crime, pollution)

i. Increase in flexible work arrangements

j. Increased private sector involvement in outdoor recreational services — camps, tours, concessions, and so on

### 4. *What major changes can be expected in the relevant social environments in the future?*

a. Growth in environmentalism and conservation ethic

b. Acceptance of diversity/cultural pluralism/ethnicity

    c. Social pressures due to further erosion of the nuclear family, delinquency, homelessness

    d. Resurgence in emphasis on education, lifelong learning

    e. Increase in voluntarism

    f. Increased availability of day-care services in work environments and higher demand for children centers in shopping areas and parks

    g. Smaller families, smaller houses, children more highly valued

    h. Explosion in do-it-yourself projects and recreation

5. *What major changes can be expected in the relevant political environments in the future?*

    a. Taxpayer revolts, which limit the ability of governments to increase taxes and thereby erodes the delivery of social services

    b. Devolution of power in all social programs, including parks and recreation, from federal to state authorities

    c. Greater use and development of federal lands

    d. Increased federal standard setting for safety and environmental protection in parklands

    e. Large increase in federal wilderness preservations, with designated environmental risk areas

    f. Shifts in public parks to self-financed programs with much heavier user fees

    g. More cooperation between public agencies, including joint programs, information sharing, and multipurpose land use

6.   *What major changes can be expected in the relevant technological environments in the future?*

a.  Safe chemical or electrical enhancement of pleasure centers of the brain

b.  Increased environmental threats to public lands from pollution, use of pesticides

c.  Computerization of park reservations and services

d.  Alternative recreational technologies, especially in the home, for example, high-resolution and two-way television

e.  Technological advancements in recreational equipment and access, for example, power skis, helicopter access, solar devices

7.   *What major changes can be expected in other external environments that could affect your organization in the future?*

a.  Privatization of many functions in parks and recreation, increased contracting for services and facilities

b.  Greater movement of recreation personnel between private and public sectors

c.  Increased use of volunteers, prison labor, probationers in parks

d.  Development of a State Conservation Corps

8.   *Which future developments would have the most impact on your choice of vision, and what are the probabilities of these high-priority developments actually occurring?*

The most critical future developments for the Department of Parks and Recreation (reworded to make them more precise) and their probabilities of occurring (on a scale of 0 to 100) by the year 2000 might be those shown in Table A.2.

## Building Scenarios

Many scenarios for the State Department of Parks and Recreation could be derived from Table A.2, among them the following.

### Scenario 1. High Economic Stress, 2005

The state and the nation have been experiencing difficult economic circumstances for well over a decade. Several years of corporate downsizing in the early 1990s improved the short-term profitability of many companies but did little to improve their long-term global competitiveness. Instead, the waves of layoffs and restructuring weakened the economy further, and it was only with great good fortune that a serious depression was averted (3a). In the absence of strong measures to improve productivity and develop the skills of the work force, businesses continued to decline until the American marketplace ranked a distant third to the robust European and Asian markets, and the United States remained dominant in weapons only, much as the ailing Soviet economy had done in the 1970s.

One of the most serious aspects of the weakened U.S. economy was that real estate and stock market prices fell, thereby substantially reducing the real (that is, inflation-adjusted) wealth of the average citizen (3b). With unemployment remaining stubbornly high for long periods, job sharing and part-time work became common. However, many workers were unable to savor the extra time as leisure, since they found themselves with two and sometimes three jobs just to make ends meet (3c). The economic stress increased social pressures, making the nuclear family a vanishing species and adding to already formidable problems of delinquency, homelessness, and other societal dysfunctions (4c). With smaller families, smaller houses, and smaller incomes, children were

Table A.2. High-Impact Developments and Their Probabilities
for the State Department of Parks and Recreation.

|  | Probability |
|---|---|
| 1. The proportion of users concerned about health and wellness aspects of recreation, as opposed to diversion or amusement, at least doubles (1a) | 80 |
| 2. The demand by elderly people for active recreation to preserve vitality and fill time available due to early retirement increases by at least 5 percent per year (1f) | 40 |
| 3. The number of foreign and out-of-state visitors to state park facilities goes up at least 50 percent (2b) | 60 |
| 4. Increased immigration, cultural pluralism, and a heightened sense of ethnic identity create significant new demands on park facilities. Such demands include soccer fields, ethnic foods in parks, and trail signs in several languages. (2d, 4b) | 70 |
| 5. A substantial growth in environmentalism and the conservation ethic makes these responsibilities equal in priority to providing recreation on state lands (4a) | 90 |
| 6. Theme parks and other man-made destination resorts in the state grow to accommodate at least 70 percent more visitors (2m) | 60 |
| 7. Taxpayer revolts limit the ability of governments to increase taxes and erode capacity to deliver all social services, including recreation (5a) | 95 |
| 8. Cooperation between public agencies, including joint programs, information sharing, and multipurpose land use, becomes standard practice for the state agency (5g) | 90 |
| 9. Privatization of many functions in parks and recreation; contracting for services and facilities with the private sector at least doubles (7a) | 40 |
| 10. Use of volunteers, prison labor, people on probation, and other unpaid workers increases by at least 50 percent in state parks (7c) | 60 |

more highly prized by those who had them, even though parents had less time to spend with kids (4g).

These forces had profound effects on recreational choices. The demand for family-oriented recreation increased as smaller families and dual-career families made parents long for "quality time" with their children (2a). With limited budgets, families were forced to be more self-reliant in all activities, which, in recreation, translated into more low-cost camping and other do-it-yourself experiences (4h). Younger adults, pressed for time as well as money, sought thrills in riskier recreation activities such as rock climbing, white-water rafting, and bungee jumping (1b).

Public agencies responsible for park and recreational services responded in various ways to the economic stress. Budgets were tightened (2f), of course, as tax revolts prevented tax increases from keeping up with the expanding demand for parks and recreational services (2q). Taxpayers simply felt that the critical needs in education, criminal justice, and economic development were of higher priority (2r). Some public recreational services were privatized to save money (2l), and the private sector became increasingly involved in outdoor recreational services such as camps, tours, concessions, and so on (3j). With much larger crowds seeking inexpensive vacations and many pursuing riskier activities, safety and security on public lands became a major requirement (1e). To economize on public funding, many programs became self-financed through user fees (5f), maintenance was perpetually deferred, and free labor — volunteers, prisoners, people on probation — was avidly sought in public parks (7c). A small but active State Conservation Corps (7d) was also established. Public agencies were under constant pressure to be innovative, to economize, and to preserve public lands for future generations.

### Scenario 2. *Shift in Values, 2005*

The U.S. economy, while not returning to its most robust days, had managed to hold its own in international competition. The recession and cutbacks of the early 1990s made American companies hungry, aggressive, and more competitive, and the weakening of the U.S. dollar in the mid 1990s increased the relative attractiveness of U.S. goods in world markets. Investments by the federal and state governments on infrastructure and education, especially in urban areas (2j), created new jobs and set the stage for productivity increases at the turn of the century. Smaller, entrepreneurial businesses were among the prime beneficiaries (3e).

With the aging of the population and fewer young workers coming into the labor force, the size of the active work force declined relative to the entire population (3f). Workers sought more flexible work arrangements to allow them to use leisure time more productively (3i) and demanded more employer-sponsored recreational programs (2o). Powerful, highly portable computers and telecommunications equipment allowed many workers to combine recreation with job-related activities, thus dispersing the work force (3h) and increasing the time available for visiting public recreation facilities (1g). Elderly people especially became far more interested in active recreation to preserve their vitality and fill time available due to early retirement (1f).

In these circumstances, social values shifted to favor a higher quality of life. There was increasing interest in education and lifelong learning as part of a general trend toward personal growth and development (4d). The average citizen expressed more concern for the health and wellness aspects of recreation, as opposed to diversion or amusement (1a). Also, the quality and intensity of the recreational experience increased in importance as people sought to develop new skills and grow in their understanding and appreciation of nature (1d). Environmentalism became a mainstream value, and strong support was available for conservation efforts (4a). People accepted and respected ethnic diversity and cultural pluralism (4b).

In response to these values, many alternative recreational opportunities became available. The number and size of theme parks and other man-made destination resorts increased (2m); scouting programs expanded to occupy the after-school time of kids of working parents (2n); and the leisure-oriented activities of community colleges and other educational institutions expanded (2p). Corporations rushed to the market with alternative recreational products for the home, such as new exercise devices and high-resolution and two-way television (6d), as well as technological advances in recreational equipment, such as power skis, helicopter access to ski areas, and a variety of solar devices for camping (6e).

The public sector responded to these new demands and values. At the federal level, for example, there was a large increase in wilderness preservation programs, with specially designated environmental risk areas (5e). Federal agencies rushed to set new standards for safety and environmental protection in parklands (5d). At the state level, recreational programs of all sorts were greatly expanded. The heightened sense of ethnic identity and diversity was recognized by responses such as soccer fields for Hispanic people, ethnic foods in parks, and trail signs in several languages (2d). Family values were recognized in the provision of children's camps and day-care centers in public parks (4f). In addition, there was greater recognition of the rights of disabled people to access to the full range of recreational opportunities (2e). Recreation had finally come to be recognized as a vital element in public health and welfare.

### Scenario 3. Government Revisionism, 2005

By the mid 1990s, social conditions had gotten so bad in the United States that the electorate was ready for a new wave of governmental activism. All the unsolved problems of drugs, crime, pollution, deteriorating roads, a failed education system, and a weakening world competitive stance combined to change voters' view (held for more than two decades) that government was the problem. Voters began to demand more public services and were willing to tax themselves a moderate amount to pay for them.

One area of considerable concern was environmental threats of all sorts (6b). Almost every day, there were newspaper stories about a new problem: loss of a rare species, excessive logging and erosion on recreational lands, acid rain, pollution of streams and rivers, and so on. Thus, while the government was committed to greater use and development of all public lands (5c), it was increasingly called on to balance water, timber, mining, and oil-drilling interests with environmental considerations in deciding on recreational uses of public lands (2k).

At the state level, recreational activities became more closely tied to other state objectives and needs. For example, the increased importance of tourism to the state's economy made it necessary to accommodate large numbers of foreign and out-of-state visitors in park facilities (2b). There was also a greater need for recreational opportunities close to urban areas (1c) and for special facilities for those with special needs.

All this led to much more cooperation between public agencies at the federal, state, and local levels on land management and protection (2g), including joint programs, information sharing, and multipurpose land use (5g). Many new powers devolved from the federal to the state level (5b), and the state had a stronger voice in the uses of federal lands (2h). In addition, there was much greater collaboration between the public and private sectors in recreational services, prompting a freer movement of personnel between the two sectors (7b). In short, a new spirit of governmental activism promised an era of renewal and innovation in the delivery of public recreational services.

### Drawing Implications

As illustrated in the Prime Pet Foods example, scenarios often stimulate thoughts about new directions for an organization that build on its strengths. The director of the State Department of Parks and Recreation might review the above scenarios and reason as follows.

### Scenario 1. High Economic Stress

*1.* With tough economic times, the department is likely to suffer disproportionate decreases in its budget. This means we'll have to do more with less. Perhaps we'd better begin soon to seek authorization to raise user fees and impose them on some activities that have so far been free. Also, we'll have to form long-term partnerships with other federal, state, and local agencies to share costs and avoid duplication of services.

2.    Privatization of some recreational functions and services would be almost mandatory in this scenario. We might be able to expand our current food concession activities to include private contracting for transportation, field guides, patrols, and equipment rental. Maybe we could even lease entire parks (like the areas around state reservoirs) or at least large areas of state parks to the private or nonprofit sectors and allow them considerable freedom to manage them without state personnel at all.

3.    If there is a great increase in demand for low-cost–family-oriented recreation, then we may need to make some major changes in the services we offer. For example, we may need to add day care or summer-camp-like experiences for youngsters, special attractions for families, and better safety protection. In fact, locating lost children and providing better fire protection could become troublesome, resource-consuming challenges for the department.

4.    The notion of a voluntary State Conservation Corps may be feasible if we start building constituencies for it right away. Though we'd promote it as a way to provide young people with volunteer opportunities in a healthful outdoor environment, its benefit to the department is that it would enable many labor-intensive functions like trail maintenance, tour guiding, and environmental protection to be done at much lower cost to the state.

### Scenario 2.  Shift in Values

1.    If quality of life becomes the dominant value in society, our department could move from being a more or less marginal state agency to one of central importance. Perhaps we

need to capitalize on our role in promoting individual wellness and environmental protection, as opposed to our current orientation to traditional recreational and amusement purposes.

2.    The flexibility that some people have in working arrangements many have to be matched by greater flexibility in the way we offer state recreational services, ranging from more hours of availability to increased services in the off-seasons. For example, perhaps we should consider special services for users of state facilities who wish to work part time while in the recreational setting through telecommuting to their offices.

3.    In this scenario, we will be called on to deliver many more services tailored to special needs—of various ethnic groups, the disabled, inner-city dwellers, and so on. Instead of considering this a problem, perhaps we should feature our response as a distinctive competence. We might then be able to earn the support of powerful lobbying groups and become eligible for federal and charitable grants that could supplement our budget.

4.    With larger populations of retired people, many of them younger and more vigorous than in earlier generations (and also more affluent), we will need to expand our services for senior citizens. That could mean modifying some of the structures on state lands, providing easier access to emergency medical care, and adding more patrols, safety precautions, and trail guides. However, perhaps some of these services could be provided on a fee-for-service basis, at least for tours and groups of senior citizens.

### Scenario 3. Government Revisionism

1.    If people seek more government services and are willing to pay for them through taxes, recreational services will be among those demanded, but only if we are able to prove and advertise their relevance and usefulness as part of a full life. So

far, self-promotion has been one of our weaknesses, and if we continue this way, we would probably not be a beneficiary of the developments described in this scenario. We need expanded public education programs to begin immediately.

**2.** To enhance the value of our department to taxpayers and the state legislature, we could tie our activities to those of other state agencies already viewed as vital, especially those concerned with environmental issues, tourism, and transportation.

**3.** Perhaps we should start joint activities with other agencies and promote various collaborative arrangements with the private sector as soon as possible. We could start by forming an advisory board with broad representation from these groups and seeking joint venture opportunities.

These ideas all contain the seeds of a potential new vision for the department, which will finally take shape in the next section.

# THE VISION CHOICE

In a complete analysis, this final section would start with mapping the full domain of services and users exactly like the product/market matrix shown in Table 6.1 in Chapter Six. Along the left-hand side of the matrix would be a list of all the services available through the department — swimming, sports, sightseeing, camping, bicycling, hiking, backpacking, fishing, hunting, boating, horseback riding, rock climbing, and so on — as well as education, outreach, environmental protection and conservation, and so forth. Across the top would be all the user groups served by the department, perhaps broken down by age (children, young adults, families, senior citizens), ethnicity, and by various other categories (tourists, the disabled, scout troops, schools, economically disadvantaged individuals). Because of its obvious size and complexity, such a matrix, while recommended for a complete analysis, is omitted here.

We will start by stating some alternative directions the department could take in the future. Of the dozens of choices available, suppose the following alternatives seemed most attractive:

The State Department of Parks and Recreation intends to make enormous progress over the next decade by . . .

1.  Becoming the most efficient agency of its kind in the country, offering the greatest amount of public recreational services per budgeted dollar of all the states

2.  Being the "Wellness Agency," dedicated to healing the ills of an urban society by contributing to physical, mental, and spiritual wellness of the citizens through the restorative power of high-quality recreational experiences

3.  Stressing access and diversity of users, especially by providing recreational services to special groups ill served by other public agencies — disabled, impoverished, or homeless people, delinquents, ethnic minorities, and others underserved by the social welfare system

4.  Emphasizing the preservation and enhancement of public lands and their natural environments while providing for current recreational needs

5.  Becoming family centered, specializing in the design of inexpensive, safe, and enriching recreational programs for the entire family

6.  Stimulating the development of private and nonprofit sector recreational programs through a variety of joint arrangements, including leasing of public lands, privatization of many public recreational activities, and joint public/private partnerships

7. Reducing the public cost of recreational services by instituting fee-for-service programs whenever possible and developing other innovative means to develop financial support for recreation

8. Stressing local empowerment and an urban focus by devolving state management authority for recreational services to regional and local authorities and acting mainly as the standard setter, facilitator, funder, educator, and planner for the state recreational system — but not actually delivering the services

With these visions identified, the next step is to test them against the criteria for an effective vision, as shown in Tables A.3 and A.4 (which use the same measures as Tables 6.2 and 6.3).

The next step is to test the alternatives against the measures of success identified earlier in the Appendix:

Public Satisfaction

- Breadth of participation

- Decrease in frustration, complaint letters

Table A.3. How Good Are the Vision Statements?

| Criteria | Alternatives | | | | | | | |
|---|---|---|---|---|---|---|---|---|
| | 1 | 2 | 3 | 4 | 5 | 6 | 7 | 8 |
| Future oriented? | 4 | 5 | 4 | 5 | 3 | 4 | 5 | 2 |
| Utopian? | 5 | 4 | 4 | 5 | 3 | 3 | 5 | 3 |
| Appropriate? | 4 | 4 | 3 | 5 | 2 | 2 | 3 | 2 |
| Reflects high ideals? | 4 | 5 | 4 | 5 | 3 | 3 | 3 | 3 |
| Clarifies purpose? | 4 | 5 | 4 | 3 | 3 | 3 | 5 | 3 |
| Inspires enthusiasm? | 4 | 5 | 4 | 4 | 3 | 4 | 3 | 2 |
| Reflects uniqueness? | 4 | 4 | 3 | 3 | 2 | 3 | 3 | 2 |
| Ambitious? | 3 | 5 | 4 | 4 | 4 | 4 | 4 | 3 |

Table A.4. Vision Statements with Weighted Criteria.

| Criteria | Relative Weight | Alternatives | | | | | | | |
|---|---|---|---|---|---|---|---|---|---|
| | | 1 | 2 | 3 | 4 | 5 | 6 | 7 | 8 |
| Future oriented? | (7) | 28 | 35 | 28 | 35 | 21 | 28 | 35 | 14 |
| Utopian? | (9) | 45 | 36 | 36 | 45 | 27 | 27 | 45 | 27 |
| Appropriate? | (8) | 32 | 32 | 24 | 40 | 16 | 16 | 24 | 16 |
| Reflects high ideals? | (9) | 36 | 45 | 36 | 45 | 27 | 27 | 27 | 27 |
| Clarifies purpose? | (10) | 40 | 50 | 40 | 30 | 30 | 30 | 50 | 30 |
| Inspires enthusiasm? | (9) | 36 | 45 | 36 | 36 | 27 | 36 | 27 | 18 |
| Reflects uniqueness? | (6) | 24 | 24 | 18 | 18 | 12 | 18 | 18 | 12 |
| Ambitious? | (7) | 21 | 35 | 28 | 28 | 28 | 28 | 28 | 21 |
| Totals | | 262 | 302 | 246 | 277 | 188 | 210 | 254 | 165 |

## Public Good

- Public health — physical and mental wellness
- Improved quality of life
- Natural resource preservation
- Enhanced tourism

## Accessibility of Services and Facilities

- Convenience
- Affordability for users
- Equity — fairness of distribution

## Efficiency of Service Delivery

- High value, reasonable cost
- Productivity of state employees and contractors

## Service Quality

- Safety

- Adequacy of maintenance
- Enhanced cultural values

Collaboration

- Cooperation with federal agencies
- Cooperation with other state and local agencies
- Cooperation with private and nonprofit sectors

These criteria are used in Tables A.5 and A.6 to compare the effectiveness of the alternatives, exactly as it was done for Prime Pet Foods in Tables 6.4 and 6.5 in Chapter Six.

Next, each alternative must be measured against key organizational factors. These tests are shown in Tables A.7 and A.8.

Finally, all the weighted scores in Tables A.4, A.6, and A.8 are totaled, as shown in Table A.9. By these criteria, alternatives 1, 2, and 4 are closely matched (and are far ahead of the other contenders). These were the following:

1. Becoming the most efficient agency of its kind in the country, offering the greatest amount of public recreational services per budgeted dollar of all the states

Table A.5. Comparing Alternatives with Measures of Success.

| Measures of Success | Alternatives | | | | | | | |
|---|---|---|---|---|---|---|---|---|
| | 1 | 2 | 3 | 4 | 5 | 6 | 7 | 8 |
| Public acceptance | 5 | 5 | 3 | 4 | 4 | 3 | 3 | 4 |
| Public good | 3 | 5 | 4 | 5 | 4 | 3 | 2 | 3 |
| Accessibility | 5 | 3 | 4 | 3 | 4 | 3 | 3 | 5 |
| Efficiency | 5 | 3 | 3 | 3 | 3 | 5 | 4 | 3 |
| Quality | 3 | 4 | 3 | 4 | 4 | 3 | 4 | 3 |
| Collaboration | 4 | 4 | 4 | 4 | 4 | 5 | 3 | 5 |

Table A.6. Weighted Comparisons with Measures of Success.

| Measures of Success | Relative Weight | Alternatives | | | | | | | |
|---|---|---|---|---|---|---|---|---|---|
| | | 1 | 2 | 3 | 4 | 5 | 6 | 7 | 8 |
| Public acceptance | (9) | 45 | 45 | 27 | 36 | 36 | 27 | 27 | 36 |
| Public good | (9) | 27 | 45 | 36 | 45 | 36 | 27 | 18 | 27 |
| Accessibility | (8) | 40 | 24 | 32 | 24 | 32 | 24 | 24 | 40 |
| Efficiency | (7) | 35 | 21 | 21 | 21 | 21 | 35 | 28 | 21 |
| Quality | (8) | 24 | 32 | 24 | 32 | 32 | 24 | 32 | 24 |
| Collaboration | (6) | 24 | 24 | 24 | 24 | 24 | 30 | 18 | 30 |
| Totals | | 195 | 191 | 164 | 182 | 181 | 167 | 147 | 178 |

**2.** Being the "Wellness Agency," dedicated to healing the ills of an urban society by contributing to the physical, mental, and spiritual wellness of the citizens through the restorative power of high-quality recreational experiences

**4.** Emphasizing the preservation and enhancement of public lands and their natural environments while providing for current recreational needs

Table A.7. Comparing Alternatives on Organizational Synergy.

| Consistency with | Alternatives | | | | | | | |
|---|---|---|---|---|---|---|---|---|
| | 1 | 2 | 3 | 4 | 5 | 6 | 7 | 8 |
| Organization's culture and values | 3 | 4 | 3 | 5 | 3 | 2 | 3 | 2 |
| Organization's strengths | 4 | 3 | 2 | 4 | 2 | 2 | 4 | 2 |
| Stakeholder needs | | | | | | | | |
| User communities | 5 | 5 | 4 | 5 | 4 | 4 | 2 | 2 |
| Governmental providers of services | 5 | 3 | 4 | 5 | 4 | 2 | 4 | 4 |
| Nongovernmental providers of services | 4 | 4 | 5 | 4 | 4 | 5 | 4 | 5 |
| Special interests | 5 | 5 | 5 | 3 | 4 | 5 | 3 | 4 |
| Taxpayers | 5 | 4 | 4 | 4 | 4 | 4 | 5 | 3 |
| Scenarios of the future | | | | | | | | |
| High economic stress | 5 | 3 | 3 | 3 | 4 | 4 | 5 | 2 |
| Shift in values | 3 | 5 | 5 | 5 | 5 | 4 | 4 | 3 |
| Government revisionism | 4 | 3 | 3 | 4 | 3 | 4 | 5 | 4 |

Table A.8. **Weighted Comparisons on Organizational Synergy.**

| Consistency with | Relative Weight | Alternatives | | | | | | | |
|---|---|---|---|---|---|---|---|---|---|
| | | 1 | 2 | 3 | 4 | 5 | 6 | 7 | 8 |
| Organization's culture and values | (10) | 30 | 40 | 30 | 50 | 30 | 20 | 30 | 20 |
| Organization's strengths | (8) | 32 | 24 | 16 | 32 | 16 | 16 | 32 | 16 |
| Stakeholder needs | | | | | | | | | |
| User communities | (9) | 45 | 45 | 36 | 45 | 36 | 36 | 18 | 18 |
| Governmental providers of services | (8) | 40 | 24 | 32 | 40 | 32 | 16 | 32 | 32 |
| Nongovernmental providers of services | (7) | 28 | 28 | 35 | 28 | 28 | 35 | 28 | 35 |
| Special interests | (7) | 35 | 35 | 35 | 21 | 28 | 35 | 21 | 28 |
| Taxpayers | (8) | 40 | 32 | 32 | 32 | 32 | 32 | 40 | 24 |
| Scenarios of the future | | | | | | | | | |
| High economic stress | (9) | 45 | 27 | 27 | 27 | 36 | 36 | 45 | 18 |
| Shift in values | (8) | 24 | 40 | 40 | 40 | 40 | 32 | 32 | 24 |
| Government revisionism | (5) | 20 | 15 | 15 | 20 | 15 | 20 | 25 | 20 |
| Totals | | 339 | 310 | 298 | 335 | 293 | 278 | 303 | 235 |

It remains now to package these into an attractive vision statement for the department. Here are some possibilities:

In the coming decade, the State Department of Parks and Recreation will...

1. Strive to at least double the number of users of state parks and recreational areas without increased funding while

Table A.9. **Summing the Evaluations of Alternatives.**

| Totals from | Alternatives | | | | | | | |
|---|---|---|---|---|---|---|---|---|
| | 1 | 2 | 3 | 4 | 5 | 6 | 7 | 8 |
| Table A.4 | 262 | 302 | 246 | 277 | 188 | 210 | 254 | 165 |
| Table A.6 | 195 | 191 | 164 | 182 | 181 | 167 | 147 | 178 |
| Table A.8 | 339 | 310 | 298 | 335 | 293 | 278 | 303 | 235 |
| Totals | 796 | 803 | 708 | 794 | 662 | 655 | 704 | 578 |

preserving the quality of the natural environment, the facilities, and the services provided (emphasizes alternative 1)

2. Become known as the state "Wellness Agency" by markedly enhancing the physical, mental, and spiritual wellness of the state's population through enriching recreational opportunities in well-preserved natural environments (emphasizes alternative 2)

3. Expand, protect, and preserve the public lands and facilities entrusted to its care so as to provide the finest recreational opportunities in the nation, now and in the future, to state residents and visitors (emphasizes alternative 4)

4. Demonstrably enrich the lives and improve the wellness of more citizens each year by providing attractive, inexpensive recreational opportunities in beautiful, well-preserved natural environments (a bit more pizazz)

The reader is invited to invent other combinations of these ideas and to search for metaphors that satisfy the requirements for an effective vision. Here again, the vision sets certain priorities, consciously chooses to deemphasize others (for example, privatization, devolution of authority), and provides a focus for strategies and decisions for years to come.

# REFERENCES

Abrams, G. "Carving Out a New Virginny." *Los Angeles Times*, Feb. 23, 1990, p. E1.

Bennett, L. *What Manner of Man.* Chicago: Johnson, 1964.

Bennis, W. *On Becoming a Leader.* Reading, Mass.: Addison-Wesley, 1989.

Bennis, W., and Nanus, B. *Leaders: The Strategies for Taking Charge.* New York: HarperCollins, 1985.

Block, P. *The Empowered Manager: Positive Political Skills at Work.* San Francisco: Jossey-Bass, 1987.

Botkin, J. W., Elmandjra, M., and Malitza, M. *No Limits to Learning: Bridging the Human Gap.* Elmsford, N.Y.: Pergamon Press, 1979.

Brown, L., and others. *State of the World, 1992.* Washington, D.C.: Worldwatch Institute, 1992.

Byrne, J. A. "Profiting from the Nonprofits." *Business Week*, Mar. 26, 1990, p. 72.

Charlier, M. "First Principle: Ailing College Treats Student as

Customer, and Soon Is Thriving." *Wall Street Journal*, July 17, 1991, p. A5.

Coates, J. F. *What Futurists Believe*. Mt. Airy, Md.: Lomond, 1989.

Confucius. In W. Safire and L. Safire, *Leadership*. New York: Simon & Schuster, 1990, p. 170.

Davis, S., and Davidson, B. *2020 Vision*. New York: Simon & Schuster, 1991.

DePree, M. *Leadership Is an Art*. New York: Doubleday, 1989.

Drucker, P. F. *The New Realities*. New York: HarperCollins, 1989.

Durant, W., and Durant, A. *The Age of Napoleon*. New York: Simon & Schuster, 1975.

Eliot, T. S. "Burnt Norton." In L. Untermeyer (ed.), *Modern American Poetry*. Orlando, Fla.: Harcourt Brace Jovanovich, 1950, 421–422.

Gardner, H. *Art, Mind and Brain: A Cognitive Approach to Creativity*. New York: Basic Books, 1982.

Halberstam, D. *The Powers That Be*. New York: Dell, 1979.

Harburgh, Y. Song composed for the film *Finian's Rainbow*. Starring F. Astaire, directed by F. Ford Coppola, 1968.

Hill, C.W.L., and Jones, G. R. *Strategic Management: An Integrated Approach*. Boston: Houghton Mifflin, 1989.

Hofstadter, D. R. *Gödel, Escher, Bach: An Eternal Golden Braid*. New York: Vintage Books, 1980.

Holmes, O. W. In W. Safire and L. Safire, *Leadership*. New York: Simon & Schuster, 1990, p. 22.

Kempe, F. "German Giant: Helmut Kohl Takes Europe's Center Stage, Surprising His Critics." *Wall Street Journal*, Nov. 30, 1990, p. A1.

Kennedy, J. F. Inaugural Address, Jan. 20, 1961.

Kidder, T. *The Soul of a New Machine*. Boston: Little, Brown, 1981.

Kouzes, J. M., and Posner, B. Z. *The Leadership Challenge: How to Get Extraordinary Things Done in Organizations*. San Francisco: Jossey-Bass, 1987.

Leavitt, H. J. *Corporate Pathfinders*. Homewood, Ill.: Dow Jones-Irwin, 1986.

*Manufacturing U.S.A.: Industry Analyses, Statistics and Leading Companies*. Detroit: Gale Research, 1989.

Mead, M. "Towards More Vivid Utopias." In G. Kateb (ed.), *Utopia*. New York: Atherton Press, 1971.

Moody, F. "Mr. Software." *New York Times Magazine*, Aug. 25, 1991, p. 26.

Naisbitt, J., and Aburdene, P. *Megatrends 2000*. New York: William Morrow, 1990.

Nanus, B. "QUEST—Quick Environmental Scanning Technique." *Long Range Planning*, Apr. 1982, pp. 39–46.

Nanus, B. *The Leader's Edge: The Seven Keys to Leadership in a Turbulent World*. Chicago: Contemporary Books, 1989.

Pascarella, P., and Frohman, M. A. *The Purpose-Driven Organization: Unleashing the Power of Direction and Commitment*. San Francisco: Jossey-Bass, 1989.

*Pet Food Institute Fact Sheet, 1990*. Washington, D.C.: Pet Food Institute, 1991.

Peters, T. *Thriving on Chaos*. New York: Knopf, 1987.

Polak, F. *The Image of the Future* (E. Boulding, trans.), Volume 2. Amsterdam: A. W. Sijhoff, 1961.

Quinn, J. B., Mintzberg, H., and James, R. M. *The Strategy Process*. Englewood Cliffs, N.J.: Prentice-Hall, 1988.

Reardon, K. K. *Persuasion in Practice*. Newbury Park, Calif.: Sage, 1991.

Richardson, J. M., Jr. (ed.). *Making It Happen: A Positive Guide to the Future*. Washington, D.C.: U.S. Association for the Club of Rome, 1982.

Rico, G. L. *Writing the Natural Way: Using Right Brain Techniques to Release Your Expressive Powers*. Los Angeles: Tarcher, 1983.

Rilke, R. M. In R. Bly, *Iron John*. Reading, Mass.: Addison-Wesley, 1990, p. 49.

Rowe, A. J., Mason, R. O., Dickel, K. E., and Snyder, N. H.

*Strategic Management: A Methodological Approach.* Reading, Mass.: Addison-Wesley, 1989.

Safire, W. "Bush's Cabinet: Who's Up, Who's Down." *New York Times Magazine,* Mar. 25, 1990, p. 31.

Schwartz, P. *The Art of the Long View.* New York: Doubleday, 1991.

Shekerjian, D. *Uncommon Genius.* New York: Viking Penguin, 1990.

Teilhard de Chardin, P. *The Future of Man.* New York: HarperCollins, 1964. (Originally published 1959.)

Thomas, B. *Walt Disney: An American Tradition.* New York: Simon & Schuster, 1976.

Thompson, A. A., and Strickland, A. J. *Strategic Management: Concepts & Cases.* Homewood, Ill.: Dow Jones-Irwin, 1990.

Trachtenberg, J. A. "Fighting the Tide, Owner Tries to Revive Big Department Store." *Wall Street Journal,* Aug. 14, 1991, p. A1.

Tregoe, B. B., Zimmerman, J. W., Smith, R. A., and Tobia, P. M. *Vision in Action.* New York: Simon & Schuster, 1989.

Watkins, B. T. "Successful Colleges Found Headed by Presidents Who Are People-Oriented, Doggedly Persistent." *Chronicle of Higher Education,* June 4, 1986, p. 20.

Yeats, W. B. "Among School Children." In R. J. Finnerman (ed.), *The Poems of W. B. Yeats: A New Edition.* New York: Macmillan, 1956 [1928].

Yukl, G. A. *Leadership in Organizations.* Englewood Cliffs, N.J.: Prentice-Hall, 1989.

# INDEX

learning about, 184; learning by, 158–164; mission of, 31, 46, 190–191; operations of, 50–56, 193; position of, 49, 114, 115, 191–192; setting for, 47–49; shared vision for, 58–59, 195; skill development in, 149; stakeholders for, 62–70, 196–201, 204–206; strategy of, 54–56; strengths and weaknesses of, 54–55, 193; success factors for, 49–50; support systems of, 59, 195; synergy in, 124–125, 222–223; and technology, 175; in twenty-first century, 173–177; uniqueness of, and vision, 29; value from, 46–47, 161, 191; vision in life cycle of, 9–10

O'Toole, J., 167

Ownership, and visionary leadership, 165–166

**P**

Parks and Recreation, Department of, visionary leadership of, 190–224

Pascarella, P., 137

Perot, H. R., 11, 166

Personifying vision, for implementation, 138–141

Peters, T., 141

Philadelphia, store's vision choice in, 128

Plato, 8

Polak, F., 8

Polaroid: organizational culture of, 50; position of, 49; and re-visioning, 157–158

Political environment: changes in, 89–90; for public sector, 207, 213–214, 216–217

Poncet, J. F., 133–134

Posner, B. Z., 4, 135–136, 137

Prime Pet Foods: alternative visions for, 119–120, 121–125; critical developments for, 93–96; defining business of, 46–49;

as example, 36–37; future developments for, 85–91; mid-level leadership for, 155; operations of, 51–56; packaging vision choice for, 126–128; product/market matrix for, 118; scenarios for, 97–108; stakeholders of, 63–70; vision audit for, 57–59; vision boundaries for, 71–77

Procter & Gamble, in scenario building, 103

Products and services, in future, 174–175

Progress, from vision, 24

Prophecy, and vision, 31

Prudential Bache Securities, communication at, 137

Public sector: aspects of visionary leadership for, 189–224; background on, 189–190; vision audit in, 190–195; vision choice in, 217–224; vision context in, 203–217; vision scope in, 195–203

Purpose. *See* Direction

**Q**

QUEST sessions, 168

Quinn, J. B., 54

**R**

Ralston Purina, size of, 48

Reality: testing, 61–77; and vision, 31–32, 44, 133–156, 168–169

Reardon, K. K., 135

Red Cross: organizational capital of, 144; and success factor, 49

Regis University, vision choice for, 109–111, 112

Relativity, and vision, 32

Remington Rand, and implementation, 36

Re-visioning: aspects of, 157–171; background on, 157–158; organizational learning for, 158–